AMERICAN GULAG

LAWRENCE BRUCKNER &
LUANNE BRUCKNER

Bloomington, IN   authorHOUSE™   Milton Keynes, UK

AuthorHouse™
1663 Liberty Drive, Suite 200
Bloomington, IN 47403
www.authorhouse.com
Phone: 1-800-839-8640

AuthorHouse™ UK Ltd.
500 Avebury Boulevard
Central Milton Keynes, MK9 2BE
www.authorhouse.co.uk
Phone: 08001974150

First published by AuthorHouse 3/1/2006

ISBN: 1-4259-2149-3 (sc)

Library of Congress Control Number: 2006901897

Printed in the United States of America
Bloomington, Indiana

This book is printed on acid-free paper.

To more than two million Americans,
who are wasting away
in our nation's prisons, unable to
fulfill the American dream,
and thereby dimming the light
on the hill for us all

CONTENTS

ACKNOWLEDGEMENTS   IX

FOREWORD   XI

INTRODUCTION   XIII

CHAPTER 1 -
WHAT IF SOMEONE BUILT A
PRISON AND NO ONE CAME?   1

CHAPTER 2 -
PRISON PRICE TAGS: TAXPAYER BURDEN   10

CHAPTER 3 -
POLITICS & MEDIA HYPE BEHIND RUNAWAY
PRISON GROWTH   18

CHAPTER 4 -
MANDATORY MINIMUMS   27

CHAPTER 5 -
HOUSTON, WE HAVE A PROBLEM   36

CHAPTER 6 -
RACIAL DISPARITIES   42

CHAPTER 7 -
CLEAR & PRESENT DANGER   48

CHAPTER 8 -
THE THREE WASTES OF INCARCERATION:
HUMAN, SOCIAL & MORAL   58

CHAPTER 9 -
REHABILITATION & RECIDIVISM:
THE REVOLVING DOOR   69

CHAPTER 10 -
  GENTLE JUSTICE   85

CHAPTER 11 -
  ALTERNATIVE SENTENCING OPTIONS   89

CHAPTER 12 -
  A MODEL PRISON   95

CHAPTER 13 -
  DISCUSSION POINTS   103

RESOURCES   107

Acknowledgements

The authors express their appreciation to the following people for their steadfast support, encouragement, and direct or indirect contributions to *American Gulag*.

Lewis Frosch

Honorable Todd Sieben, Illinois State Senator, 45th District

Honorable Ron Lawfer (Ret.), Illinois State Representative

Honorable Sharon Hook, Carroll County Board Chairman

Gary Heide

Fay Ashby, York Precinct Chairman

Marilyn Childs

Dr. Arthur Donart, Human Rights Activist

Tom Kocal, Prairie Advocate

Helen LaTouche, Carroll County Board

Dr. Stephan Perry

Richard Smith, Esq.

Regina Vesely

Susan Giffin, editor and researcher, and

Brianna Bruckner, their beloved daughter

We have created an American gulag.
We have 1.6 million people behind bars,
and probably two-thirds of these
in the federal system are there
for drug-related crimes.

Barry McCaffrey
National drugs czar
1996

FOREWORD

I suspect that all the crimes committed
By all the jailed criminals do not equal
In total social damage that of the
Crimes committed against them.

Karl Menninger
The Crime of Punishment
1969

Our prison population exceeds countries like Japan, China, and India often by a multiple of 10 or more per 100,000. The seven plus millions imprisoned or under other forms of corrections control are growing at a much faster rate than the population. We invest more into making them less capable than we invest in higher education. These seven plus millions are largely poor, under-educated and often lack basic necessities. Jail has become a means to get a roof over one's head and much needed healthcare. What contribution to society can we hope for from the millions of damaged people that will be released to families and communities that are unprepared for them? Forecasts of rapidly rising rates of crime appear plausible in the absence of effective re-entry programs in much of the country. In response government leaders are planning more prisons and increased investments for the failed War on Drugs.

I am afraid that anticipated government responses can only make the problem worse. We are hurtling down a path of becoming a greatly diminished country. Forty years ago Karl Menninger in his book, *The Crime of Punishment,* pointed to the deep flaws in our "corrections" systems. Instead of taking measures to correct the flaws identified by Menninger, state and national leaders responded to populist calls to get tough on crime. They have created a monster that not only threatens our competitiveness but which also poses a security threat. We have concentrated a vast army of troubled people together with hardened criminals and potential terrorists. We are beginning to see the emerging threat of terrorist gangs taught in our prisons paid for by our taxpayers at a cost per annum equal to a Harvard education. The greatest threat to our nation may lie within, in our own prisons.

What must we do? We need leadership that does not flinch from the realities of the problem. We need a strategy for transformational change that can eliminate the threat to the country from our American Gulag as so well put by Lawrence Bruckner in this remarkable book. Our "corrections" systems must be transformed to correct, producing people more able to be productive citizens than when they entered.

Lawrence Bruckner has issued a call to action. Who is listening?

Citizens for Effective Justice is dedicated to the goals outlined by Lawrence Bruckner. We believe it is possible to reduce our prison population to levels comparable to other advanced democracies within a generation. We place particular emphasis on reducing the racial imbalance in our prisons.

American Gulag presents the problems in the American criminal justice system in a clear and concise manner. For the lay reader unfamiliar with prison issues this book will be disturbing. I hope many will heed its call for action starting with their own community and join with other communities to build a national coalition that can transform a grossly wasteful system to one that again builds the strength of our country.

Harold E. Taylor
President
Citizens for Effective Justice
Bloomington, Indiana

INTRODUCTION

*The mood and temper of the public
in regards to the treatment of
crime and criminals is one of the
most unfailing tests of the
civilization of any country.*

*Winston Churchill
1910*

This book is about waste in the American criminal justice system: waste of human lives, waste of billions of dollars. Most people do not want to talk about waste. Politicians, the media, and the prison system itself, equally complicit in perpetuating the problem, look the other way when the issue of waste surfaces. People employed in the system, who might be unemployed were it not for rampant waste that gave them jobs in the first place, get all edgy and insecure when the topic of waste comes up.

The general public knows far too little about waste, especially in the U. S. criminal justice system, to have an educated opinion. But everyone who pays taxes in America should be *outraged* by the time they finish reading this book. Billions of dollars are wasted each year in this one area of government alone. Perhaps an outright revolt would result if taxpayers knew the facts about waste in all areas of government.

We shall confine our discussion to the criminal justice system, which despite billions of dollars that support it annually, is dying a slow and painful death. Like accidentally flushing a goldfish down the toilet, is there any point at which you might save it? Have we gone too far from the essence of our penal code—reformation, not vindictive justice—to right the system?

The crux of the problem goes back to the early 1980s with the passage of inflexible sentencing laws that flooded our state and federal prisons with non-violent offenders, such as drug users. Political leaders across the nation proposed get-tough legislation; legislators complied. "Lock 'em up and throw away the keys" echoed in campaigns across the land. Prisons, bursting at the seams, turned to privatization. States built more prisons faster than they could fill them, and some—like the prison in Thomson, Illinois—have stood empty for years, a major waste of taxpayer dollars.

Under political pressure to sweep the streets of criminals and fight the war on drugs, including those who did not deserve prison sentences, states turned to warehousing and away from rehabilitation. Programs that once scored significant success rates in stemming recidivism have been abandoned. The revolving doors on our prisons remain well oiled and active.

Waste includes far more than dollars. The greatest, most incalculable waste is human life—those lost to a harsh system of excessive punishment—which often does not fit the crime. Waste touches the countless lives of the families torn apart by an unjust system—by separation, shame, and suffering—when the primary breadwinner gets sucked into a protracted sentence unbefitting his crime.

Social waste comes in the form of community programs, education, and service initiatives—many sacrificed for the political expediency of supporting a thriving prison system. It comes through the added burden of more and more families dependent on state and federal assistance, and on children abandoned or left to a life on the street, priming them for a life of crime. Every time someone goes to prison, society has failed. We have failed to provide the most basic tools to keep our citizens—men and women—free, educated, and productive.

There is moral waste, too: America has long been noted as a land of freedom, but we have turned our backs on freedom as the core right—the moral right—of all Americans. Our civil liberties are vanishing day by day. When people commit non-violent crimes and receive punishment comparable to those who commit far more serious crimes, we nullify their American right to freedom. Worse still, we have become an unforgiving people. We forgive presidents and preachers, but not the poor who cannot reach the first rung of the ladder to success.

The vast majority of non-violent offenders should not be in prison at all; certainly not in maximum-security prisons, but, rather, enrolled in drug rehabilitation programs. The government evidently has not figured out how to profit by an alternative to drug trafficking and incarceration.

We face a national dilemma. Regardless how many prisons we build, there will always be persons who will threaten our safety. Every time we remove a criminal from the streets, others appear quickly. The prison system, in fact, endangers society. Most prisoners would be quick to tell how easily they learn new methods of crime and violence. Considering that most prisoners eventually are released from prison, they bring out with them new ways to commit crimes against society. Men often use the revolving doors of prisons purposefully to learn new crimes, only to put them into practice when they get out.

Young non-violent offenders thrown in a system with violent offenders and into an environment that has violent underpinnings emerge with greater tendencies toward violence. They become violent through peer pressure (or for their own survival in prison), though perhaps they were not violent in the first place.

With an average recidivism rate hovering 60 percent or higher, something is clearly wrong with our system of 'corrections'. What makes criminals return to prison within two or three years of release? Can this revolving door syndrome be halted or is it too late to change?

American Gulag presents an overview of the U.S. prison system, focusing primarily on the waste within the system that snatches the taxpayers' money and diverts it from education and redeeming social programs.

We begin by looking at one specific example of the gross waste of taxpayer funds—building the $143 million dollar state-of-the-art prison in Thomson, Illinois that five years after completion remains unoccupied. From there, we look at the cost of building prisons, in general, and the political motivation that mandates building more and more of them, regardless of crime statistics.

We observe the problems of overcrowded prisons that spawn disease and violence; we examine racial disparities and the lopsided approach to incarceration that targets the poor and the people of color. To better understand how we got into this mess, we also look at mandatory minimum sentences that removed discretion from judges and forced them to lock up prisoners longer than necessary.

We look at the pros and cons of rehabilitation and recidivism, a foreign system of gentle justice, and alternative sentencing options. We conclude with a suggestion for a model prison, offered by a man who served almost 30 years in prison, and discussion points for continuing the dialogue that leads to a call to action.

The bottom line throughout this book is waste: waste of taxpayer dollars—waste of human lives caught in the mire of an inefficient system—waste of families torn part by an unjust system—waste of money that is better spent on education and social programs in the community. And morally the waste of a system that opts to warehouse men in conditions that deny them basic human rights that renders them angry, bitter, and vengeful.

We have concentrated angry men and women in schools for crime and now increasingly for terror. Nearly 700,000 generally ill equipped prisoners are released every year to a society that shuns them. What if instead of returning to prison these men took on the mission of terror to destroy the society that has dispossessed them? There are increasingly alarming signs that terror networks are breeding in our prisons. What will these angry men do when they are released?

Those who question the use of the word *gulag* might not do so had they experienced long-term incarceration in American prisons. The Soviet gulag system under Cheka and Stalin grew to include forced labor camps housing millions of prisoners in extremely harsh conditions. Prisoners in the Soviet *gulag* did not have adequate food or sufficient clothing for extreme temperatures. They had to work long hours, endure physical abuse by camp guards, and experienced a high death rate from disease and substandard health care.

More and more, some American prisons, which warehouse men in cramped conditions, resemble the Soviet *gulag*. Improper nourishment, minimal clothing, abuse by officers, rampant disease unchecked by inadequate health care, and increased examples of wrongful deaths are commonplace.

One ray of hope comes from comparing the Soviet system *then* and our system *now*: the Soviet gulag eventually led to openness and enlightenment (*glasnost*) and the dismantling of the totalitarian state (*perestroika*). Mikhail Gorbachev introduced glasnost as a way to make the Soviet Union's management transparent and open to debate. His perestroika was a program of economic, political, and social restructuring.

The Soviets labored in camps for the good of the state. In our prison system, however, we should appropriate the gulag concept to make a paradigm shift from warehousing people to rebuilding their lives. Instead of using prisoners for the good of the state (nation), we would give them the opportunities to rebuild their lives for their own good, which ultimately is for the good of everyone.

We can only hope that the American gulag returns our country to one where freedom of speech, debate, and dissent is once again respected and where domestic economic, political, and social restructuring takes priority over wars and uninvited interference in the business of other countries around the world.

One final note: For the reader, interested in plumbing the depths of corruption in the U.S. criminal justice system, this book falls short. It is intended to reach the uninformed readers on an issue that continues to critically affect their tax dollars with no remedy in sight from leaders now in power and no hope for abatement any time soon. New leadership is needed to bring about a paradigm shift.

1

WHAT IF SOMEONE BUILT A PRISON AND NO ONE CAME?

If we can house inmates there [Thomson]
more cost effectively and in a setting
that is safer for Corrections employees,
then it's absolutely something we should do.

Abby Ottenhoff
Spokesperson for the Illinois governor

In a sandy savanna one mile from the center of the village of Thomson, Illinois stands the 1600-cell state-of-the-art Thomson Correctional Center. This $143 million maximum-security prison was completed in 2001. Although it was designed to house 1,800 inmates, five years later, it remains empty. Under former Governor Jim Edgar, the state borrowed the money through its capital bond program to build the facility, but budgetary constraints and political posturing since 9/11 have kept the state from fulfilling the prison's purpose.

For the 600 residents of Thomson, the state's decision to build a prison there infused in them a gold rush mentality. Residents of Thomson and rural northwest Carroll County had already suffered the loss of jobs with closure of an army depot. Although many communities reject the idea of having a prison in such close proximity to its town center, Thomson residents welcomed the prospects of higher employment and improved economy.

From 1998 to 2001, business owners upgraded their shops—often at the expense of a second mortgage on their homes—and entrepreneurs launched new businesses to meet the expected traffic that would come naturally with the influx of prison personnel and guests.

Some of the residents were not so excited, however. Many older people had moved to Thomson from Chicago determined to get away from urban blight. Carroll County has the second oldest population of all state counties, with 25 percent of its residents over 65. These elder people were in terrible fear because the state was bringing this massive structure with its overwhelming influx of outsiders—very, very bad people—who would be kept nearby under maximum security. Fear almost became paralysis: some of those newer elderly residents that had sought sanctuary in a rural community sold their homes to leave Thomson before the rush came.

In April 2001, when the prison was due to open, there was an air of expectation, almost like one feels with the coming of a new baby. The expected day arrives, and you're never quite ready. But there was one delay...then another...and another. A terrible depression set in. Thomson residents had kept hope alive for years. They were ultra psyched up from all the time they watched this giant prison being built in their backyards.

In 2002, another delay came with the gubernatorial campaign and promises of a new day dawning, more frustrations for Thomson. Hope stretched to the breaking point. Almost a silent desperation set in. The people had been promised so many times that the prison would open, but hopes for beefing up the economy and paring away unemployment were dashed. People went through denial, then anger and frustration, and finally, resignation. There has been no closure for the people of Thomson. The prison stands just one mile from the center of the village. The prospects that Thomson Correctional Center will open any time soon are dim indeed.

To add insult to injury, the State of Illinois pays $800,000 a year to maintain an empty prison, plus interest on the $143 million. The state spent $4 million building a new water system, so there is interest on the $4 million. And for the first two years after the prison was finished, the state paid the Thomson warden a full salary of $130,000 per year!

The village built a new sewer system, which was designed for 3,500 people. With the expected 1800 inmates and prison employees, the system requires extra water, which is wasted now because they have to pump the water even though the prison is not open.

Then there is the need for heating and cooling—heat in the winter to prevent pipes from bursting and air conditioning in the summer to keep the sensitive computers and security systems from shutting down.

At first, officers were posted at the prison to make sure no one broke into the facility. Now, only one man works there. He goes around flushing toilets, running water, checking the lights, and making sure all the systems are operational.

With an estimated $50 million appropriation needed to open the Thomson prison, Governor Rod Blagojevich in the past has gone on record that it is not possible to open Thomson or two other state prisons that remain empty or partially filled. That, despite the fact that state prisons in Illinois have run as high 168 percent capacity in recent years. Instead of utilizing these other facilities, the state has been forced to house two or three men to a cell and to fill their prisons beyond the maximum capacity.

Overcrowding has resulted in a cutback of rehabilitation and training programs that reduce recidivism. The result of this mismanagement will be that a higher percentage of released inmates from overcrowded prisons will return, imposing further direct costs. The indirect costs, including damaged families and tax revenue, are incalculable.

In his State of the State address on January 18, 2006, Governor Blagojevich made no mention of opening the prison in Thomson. In a campaign year, one would have expected him to promise he would open it, if for no other reason to garner votes. We predict that he will promise to open the prison in January 2007, campaign on that promise all summer long, and then, if he's elected, he'll find a crisis that will divert the money away from opening Thomson. If he's defeated, the new governor would have to come up with the money.

Remaining in the shadows of this vacant prison is a two-part dilemma: first is the enormous waste of taxpayer dollars to build a much needed prison yet not considering the costs of staffing and maintaining it. Second is the critical problem of overcrowding by improper usage of the state's prisons. The state has 26 prisons, some of them very old and too small to be efficient any longer. They all have administrations; wardens get paid $130,000 a year or more. So, strictly from an economic standpoint, it makes sense to close some of the smaller prisons and open a larger facility.

The Turning Point

First, to understand how Illinois got into this predicament, we must go back a number of years. Indeed, we need go back less than 50 years to see how the system changed from merely housing criminals to making incarceration a highly profitable business and an equally highly charged political plank in party platforms on both sides of the aisle.

When the Cold War started winding down during the Nixon presidency and the enemy—the Soviet Union— became a peaceful giant after all, we needed a new enemy. Governments that want to control their people rule by fear. There must always be an enemy, a booga booga, to make the people support whatever programs the government wants to enforce. Back then, criminals became the new enemy, one lurking on every street corner, behind every door.

As Ayn Rand wrote, "There is no way to rule innocent men. The only power any government has is the power to crack down on criminals. Well, when there aren't enough criminals, one makes them. One declares so many things to be a crime that it becomes impossible for men to live without breaking laws."

Enter Illinois native, Ronald Reagan, who boldly launched a crackdown on crime in America and declared war on organized crime and career criminals. "The liberal approach to coddling criminals didn't work and never will."

Reagan was "determined to cripple the drug pushers who are poisoning the minds and bodies of our children. We want mandatory sentences, we want firm and speedy application of penalties, and we want to abolish parole for federal offenses."

A card-carrying conservative, Reagan gave the country its second longest period of peace-time prosperity, but he also ushered in an era of wanton spending on criminal justice that has led us down a dark path of immense corruption, greed, and inhumanity.

Even before the burgeoning business of building prisons started 25 years ago, prisons sprung up in blighted areas to boost employment, satisfy politicians' campaign rhetoric or tempt legislators in their deliberations over state budgets. All these without considering the sudden rise in criminal convictions as justification for building more prisons. All these 'seeds in a fertile field brought forth a multi-billion-dollar industry.

In the 1980s and 1990s, when conviction laws handed down longer sentences to drug offenders and other criminals, the prison population in Illinois, for example, grew 265 percent. In 1980, the state incarcerated only 13,000, but that number swelled to almost 48,000 by 2001.

The snowballing effect of tougher laws and more convictions forced states like Illinois to build prisons faster than they could fill them. Today, more than 45,000 men and women are incarcerated in the state's 44 adult prisons, adult transition centers, work camps, and impact incarceration program facilities.

In a 2004 update of the Illinois prison population, Roger E. Walker, Jr., Director of the Illinois Department of Corrections, reported that by the end of 2004, the state's adult prison population was 35.1 percent over rated capacity. That means a total of 44,054 inmates were in a correctional system with a rated capacity of 32,609. The prison population grew 17.0 percent from 37,658 in 1995.

Walker commented on the reason for the prison population growth in his state. "Much of the prison population growth has been attributed to longer prison terms and increased court admissions due to the enactment of stricter laws, many written to enhance the penalties for drug and weapons violations. In recent years, however, the Department has seen a greater proportion of inmates sentenced to prison with shorter sentences for lower class offenses.

"There also had been an increase in admissions for released inmates who committed a technical violation while on MSR [Mandatory Supervised Release]. Lengths of stay for technical violations are relatively shorter than are those for court admissions. Instead of incarcerating more long-term inmates, the Department had been going through a period in which inmates with shorter lengths of stay were advancing more rapidly through the prison system. Consequently, the inmate population did not accumulate at rates previously associated with longer sentences. However, the effects of the long-term sentencing enhancements enacted during the late 1990s are beginning to take effect, as seen by a 1.5 percent increase in the prison population during 2004."

In 2005, there were 3,200 empty prison beds in Illinois and 45,451 prisoners crowded into cells designed for only 34,151. The DOC notes the state is operating at 34.8 percent over capacity. The Illinois Auditor General in 2005 reported that the state's prison system is "grossly overcrowded."

As of February 2004, 91 percent of Illinois' inmates lived in cells of two or more; in some situations, they are housed in spaces clearly designed for one man. In order to minimize abuse and violence in maximum-security prisons, it is important to house inmates in single cells. Yet Illinois continues to double-bunk prisoners rather than utilize prisons that are empty or partially filled.

One prisoner tells what it is like to be incarcerated at Menard Correctional Center, constructed in 1878 and designed for 1,938 maximum-security inmates, but operating with an average daily population of 3,315, according to the IDOC's Fiscal year 2003 Annual Report. He bases some of his information on the IDOC/Menard Compliance Audit.

"The ratio of guards to cons went from 1 to 4.5 in 2002 to 1 to 5.1 in 2004. This has been accomplished by the addition of an extra bed in each of the tiny seg [segregation] cages that were engineered, designed and built as one-man punishment cells. The extra bed was added without any known legislative authority or building permit. These one-man cells are just 4½ feet wide and 10 feet long. The bed is 3 feet wide. This leaves just 1½ feet of floor space alongside the bunk. Only one man can be out of bed at a time, as there is simply not enough room in the cell. Then, as if to add insult to profound injury, the mental defective that added the second bunk did not leave enough room between the two beds to allow the person to sit up on the bottom bunk."

How does the state get away with double-bunking under those conditions when the American Correctional Association (ACA), which accredits prisons, recommends 70 square feet as the minimum cell size? The answer is simple; the Menard prison—like many prisons—is old. When it was built, it produced single-cell housing, but, by necessity, it has been forced to double-cell inmates due to overcrowding today.

The prisoner responds. "In order to comply with state law, there must be 50 square feet of unencumbered floor space per man in any cell where prisoners are kept for more than 10 hours a day. The men in Menard are kept 'in cell' for 23 hours a day and must share 26 square feet of floor space, which results in just 13 square feet per prisoner. To put this into a meaningful perspective, if we were animals of the same size and weight, the ASPCA [American Society for the Prevention of Cruelty to Animals] would close this place down in a heartbeat."

The same inmate explains how the state calculates the difference, "The State compliance audit has used some mysterious 'cell size averaging technique' to come up with 38 square feet as the 'approximate square feet per inmate.' This number cannot be substantiated by any known method of computation. I really think it is complete fiction based upon the necessary empty cells that await emergencies in other prisons."

Unanswered Questions

With Illinois operating at 168 percent, some overriding questions remain unanswered: Why is the state double-bunking its prisoners? Why is it operating some prisons at a partially filled capacity? Why doesn't the state open other prisons that would ease overcrowding and relieve the tensions and problems that overcrowding creates?

State officials now admit that they overreacted to the demand for more prisons years ago. With the Illinois budget deficit soaring around $5 billion, Governor Blagojevich has flip-flopped on the subject. He stated that Illinois could save $2 million by shifting inmates in the 133-year-old Prison Correctional Center to Thomson, despite the fact that the state needs a $50 million appropriation to open and run Thomson. But when?

Although crime is down in the state and the prison population has leveled off, officials expect that to change in the coming years. The IDOC predicts an increase of 10percent (or 50,000) in the prison population by 2010.

The AFSCME [American Federation of State, County, and Municipal Employees], the union that represents corrections officers, believes Illinois should not have to close other prisons in order to open Thomson. According to union spokesman, Anders Lindall, "We need to talk about opening and fully utilizing the facilities we've got instead of closing one to open another. If it requires additional revenue to do that, that's the discussion we need to have."

The Menard prisoner holds a different opinion of the union position. "The union [AFSCME] responsible for maintaining and preserving all these [prison] jobs objects to opening Thomson prison for several reasons. First, it would be run with many fewer dues-paying guards, which means less money in the union coffers and less total clout in the State Capitol. Second, it would take jobs desperately needed in Southern Illinois and transfer them to the Northwest corner of the state. This would literally transfer over $50 million per year from Randolph County to Carroll County."

Logic holds that it makes more sense to open Thomson and ease the overcrowding in other prisons throughout Illinois. It makes sense for the prisoners and taxpayers, whose money would be more efficiently used if some of the problems of overcrowding were eliminated. It is shameful that taxpayers have paid for the construction of a prison that remains empty and local officials have been forced to support improvements to its infrastructure.

People across the board are feeling the financial pinch, from taxpayers that paid for state bonds to build it to Thomson residents who struggle to keep their businesses afloat after mortgaging their homes to improve their businesses or open new ones.

"We all hope for the day when a lack of crime would indicate that Illinois' prisons are no longer needed, but unfortunately that day has not yet come. All of Illinois' correctional facilities are necessary to ensure the well-being of the state's correctional officers and prison staff, of the inmates houses in the prisons, and of the Illinois public," said Illinois State Senator Dan Rutherford (53rd District).

Taxpayer money would be better utilized paying for a fully operational Thomson prison rather than on maintaining an empty one.

Waste Issues:

1. *Building a $143 million dollar prison without setting aside operational funding*

2. *Keeping the Thomson Correctional Center closed, despite growing needs due to overcrowding problems in other prisons in Illinois*

3. *Ineffectively using tax dollars throughout Illinois criminal justice system.*

2

PRISON PRICE TAGS: TAXPAYER BURDEN

> Prisoners are commodities, and a profit
> must be realized from commodities.
> A lot of 'good guys' make
> an easy living off us 'bad guys.'
>
> *A Pennsylvania prisoner*

Prisons are big business. The cost of building a single prison looms well over a hundred million dollars—and sometimes hundreds of millions of dollars—and the cost of operating one easily runs at several millions of dollars annually. With such plush budgets, one wonders why there is so much waste.

States are in the business of punishment, and many along the way profit big time. Nepotism and corruption are familiar cousins in a thriving industry with little meaningful oversight.

If numbers alone qualify a prison system as a gulag, then the American system should qualify. Almost 13 million people are admitted to American jails every year; in what amounts to a turnstile effect, between 10 and 11 million inmates are released from local jails annually. In addition, almost 700,000 inmates return to society from state and federal prisons each year.

According to the International Centre for Prison Studies, as of December 31, 2004, the United States led the entire world in its number of prisoners. That is not a distinction in which we should be proud. By year-end 2004, there were 2,135,901 people incarcerated in United States prisons or 724 prisoners per every 100,000 U. S. residents, based on an estimated national population of 295.1 million. That figure was up from 1,961,247 at a rate of 685 per 100,000 for 2001.

Women comprised 6.9 percent of state prison populations in 2004. The overall occupancy level of state prisons was 112 percent that year in a total of 1,558 state facilities with an official total capacity of 1,090,000.

At year end 2004, there were 3,218 black male sentenced prison inmates per 100,000 black males in the U.S., compared to 1,220 Hispanic male inmates per 100,000 Hispanic males, and 463 white male inmates per 100,000 white males.

According the Bureau of Justice statistics in 2001, approximately 57 percent of inmates were under the age 35 and 4 percent of state prison inmates were not U.S. citizens. Six percent of state prison inmates were held in private facilities (privatized prisons), and 57 percent of inmates had a high school diploma or GED equivalent. Among state prison inmates in 2000, nearly half (49 percent) were sentenced for violent crime, a fifth (20 percent) for property crime, and a fifth (21 percent) for drug crimes.

States spend more on criminal justice than municipalities, counties, and the federal government spend. The cost of corrections, including state, local, and federal corrections budgets, ran to more than $20 billion a year in the early 1990s. State governments spent nearly $59 billion on criminal and civil justice in 2001.

The cost of adding new cells to keep up with the constant demand for more space is estimated at $6 billion a year.

Prisons are expensive. Taxpayers pay an estimated $40 billion a year for prisons. Feeding and caring for a healthy inmate costs from $25,000 to $30,000 a year and double or triple that for an old, infirm prisoner. Many people reading this book do not make $25,000 a year in wages or salary. Think about it.

One new jail or prison is built in America every week, and about 7.6 million people are under some form of correctional custody, from federal prisons to probation. By 2004, there were 5,069 correctional facilities in the U.S., including 1,558 state prisons, 146 federal facilities, and 3,365 local jails. And we're not even talking yet about juvenile homes and prisons. About 7 million Americans spend at least one day in jail every year.

11

Construction costs run as high as $100,000 per cell. Gun towers cost $200,000 and must be placed 250 feet apart on the prison grounds, and two officers must be posted in each tower.

The $143 million cost of building the prison at Thomson is a fairly common price tag. The more bells and whistles that go into making these modern prisons keep pace with today's technology, the higher the bill to build them, unless private corporations build them. More on that later.

Consider the hefty price tag of $400 million California taxpayers footed in the early 1990s to build the Twin Towers Correctional Facility, the world's largest jail. Since 1980, California has built 21 new prisons to the tune of more than $5 billion and an operating cost of $4.6 billion. In 2003, the California system had 32 prisons, a prison population of 159,390, and an annual budget of $5.3 billion. The system does not work and it is driving the state towards bankruptcy.

With all the money (more than $46 billion) being spent annually by taxpayers in states across the nation, shouldn't they expect a return on their investment? Say, reduction in crime? Experts rarely offer any encouragement in this area. In fact, studies show that the 300+ percent increase in incarcerations since the late 1970s has not contributed much to the 27 percent drop in crime.

For example, in West Virginia the incarceration rate swelled by 131 percent but the crime rate dropped only 4 percent. In great contrast, Virginia—at the same time—increased their incarceration rate 28 percent, but had a crime drop of 21 percent.

It's all about who you lock up that determines any adjustment in the crime rate, according to experts. "If it's a serial rapist, that makes an impact on crime," notes Mark Mauer of the Sentencing Project in Washington, D.C. "But if it's a kid selling crack on the corner, that just creates a job opening for someone else."

Most state prison systems do not seem to concern themselves with the lack of correlation between incarcerations and crime statistics. It's bigger business to build more prisons instead.

Design-Build, a construction trade magazine, estimates that 3,300 new prisons were build in the 1990s at a cost of $27 billion with another

286 on tap valued at an additional $2.4 billion. That's just construction costs. Remember those Twin Towers that taxpayers paid for in Los Angeles to the tune of $400 million? That facility sat for more than a year because there was no money available to open and operate it.

Our entire culture has its priorities confused. In the same years (1980 to 1996) that prison spending skyrocketed in every state, spending on higher education declined in 19 of those states. In May 2001, Colorado legislators transferred $59 million tagged for improving colleges and universities to prison expansion projects.

Despite a slowly growing public voice against prisons and excessive sentences, special interest groups with a financial interest in the prison system remain committed to building more prisons and furthering their incarceration agenda. With George W. Bush, who as governor of Texas ran the second most aggressive system of locking up people in the nation (next to Louisiana), they feel assured that their voices will be heard.

Consider those groups with powerful incentives to maintain a steady, if not increasing, influx of prisoners: private, for-profit prison corporations, which have become a multibillion-dollar industry. Companies that provide health care, phones, food, and other services in correctional facilities enjoy equally the harvest of millions of dollars annually.

Small towns and hamlets, like Thomson, lobby for new prisons in their areas to boost their economies and employment rates. They would not succeed if they lobbied against incarceration, so they, too, become involved in seeing that people are locked up. The American Legislative Exchange Council, a policy group supported by private prison companies, has helped draft tougher sentencing laws across the nation, and the union that represents California corrections officers contributes millions every election to tough-on-crime candidates.

Private prisons

The most profitable industry in America today is the private prison industry. At first blush, the idea sounds like a good one. If taxpayers and state governments cannot afford to build and operate prisons, the private sector might offer a solution. And, depending on whom you talk to, it has done so. Today, 6.5 percent of inmates are in privately managed facilities.

The lion's share of the business belongs to CCA, Corrections Corporation of America, based in Nashville. Although CCA's numbers continue to grow, by 2005, they supervise more than 63,000 prisoners in almost half the country. While the concept of private prisons is not new, the idea for the modern private prison complex came from CCA.

CCA's main rival is Wackenhut, founded in 1954 by George Wackenhut, a former FBI official. Next is Cornell Companies. Base in Palm Beach Gardens, Florida, the company has divisions across the country in almost every state. They have even made the Fortune 500 list of American's Most Admired Company. As if they don't have enough business here in the U. S., they have expanded their services to several countries abroad.

To realize substantial profits, private corporations must be sure that the prisons they build will operate at 90-95 percent capacity. Investors, after all, want a return, but unlike taxpayers, they generally succeed in getting something back for their investment.

> [There is a] basic philosophical problem
> when you begin turning over
> administration of prisons to people who have
> an interest in keeping people locked up.
>
> *Jenni Gainsborough*
> *ACLU*
> *National Prison Project*

Indeed, if the guiding goal is to keep the prison population up for the sake of profits, it is no wonder that any notion of rehabilitation has been abandoned. While private companies take some of the taxpayer burden off the costs of building prisons, if there is no incentive to rehabilitate inmates in their charge, then waste remains a major factor in the system. To be sure, there is a dollar amount saved in operations, but questions abound as to how private companies effect those savings.

Some examples: lower pay rates for employees, portion control food servings, substandard medical care, discontinuation of programs for inmates, and other methods of downsizing that are harmful to prisoners. Private companies have been known to skimp on building repairs and tolerate the presence of roaches and rats.

To protect—and increase—their profit margins, private companies must cut corners on drug and alcohol rehabilitation, counseling, literacy programs, and education. In 1995, Wackenhut was investigated for diverting $700,000 intended for drug treatment programs at a Texas prison.

While private prisons protect their own profitability, they don't reduce the cost of incarceration for state governments. They merely siphon off all amenities and services from prisoners and often by hiring incompetent, unqualified corrections officers.

These waste issues are all valid criticisms of private contractors. Another criticism is that private companies, bent on keeping the population of their prisons up, boast higher intake rates than public prisons do. The more prisoners, the greater the profit.

In all fairness, not every private prison company is self-serving. Some of them, like T. Warren Investments in Houston, design and build prisons that run more efficiently and more cost effectively. One innovation there was the first grease-less prison kitchen, made possible by the use of convection ovens. The savings in cleaning costs alone were outstanding.

Tommy Warren, who once owned 28 prisons throughout Texas, introduced the idea of eliminating gun towers in minimum- and medium-security prisons and replacing them with high-tech electronic surveillance equipment that is less manpower-intensive. He also introduced the design-build concept of setting aside 25 percent of prison beds for rehabilitation.

In one facility, he developed a two-acre garden in which prisoners could work, learn, and develop successful skills that are transferable to the outside. "One day an inmate showed me a very large red ripe tomato he had just picked from the prison garden. He said, 'I never would have

Lawrence Bruckner & Luanne Bruckner

believed that I could grow such a big tomato. I can't wait now to get out and plant a garden for my grandmother.'"

From architects to academics who study the prison systems and their charges, from food service vendors to healthcare firms, from corrections bureaucrats to psychologists, there is a lot of money to be made from the proliferation of prisons. All of the major private prison companies have their own lobbyists. With legislative support come lucrative contracts.

CCA has been especially adept at expansion through political payoffs. The first prison the company managed was in its home state of Tennessee. Tennessee Governor Ned McWherter, a CCA stockholder, said in the company's 1995 annual report, "The federal government would be well served to privatize all of their corrections."

Private prison companies claim that they offer taxpayers a bargain because they operate far more cheaply than state firms do. In food service alone, officers and staff appropriate food for their own use, including outside food service businesses. Food often served to inmates is inedible—undercooked poultry, watery and tasteless vegetables, and half-spoiled fruit and milk. The amount of food thrown away by inmates on a daily basis is criminal.

Indeed, taxpayers foot the food bill for prisoners, but officers get the best of the lot, either by stealing it or eating at plentiful buffets along with the rest of the prison staff—at taxpayer expense.

Food and supplies—even kitchen equipment—is wasted, discarded, misappropriated or stolen. In each prison, one can cite staggering conditions and countless losses. In one prison, the bakery made too many cake servings. If not stolen by staff and officers, they were thrown out because prisoners are not permitted to have extras. That day, they also threw away more than 125 loaves of bread. The waste in one day for those two items exceeded $1,000. Didn't anyone there ever hear of serving leftovers the next day?

Stories like these and worse can be replicated in every prison across the country. In one prison, for instance, the food service director had her own catering business, for which she frequently appropriated food and other supplies from the prison kitchen. Officials chose not to punish her, indicating there was at least tacit approval.

According to the Menard prisoner, inmates there are fed on throwaway Styrofoam trays that are not recycled and that end up in the Illinois landfill. For that one prison alone, the State pays $1,200 per day to get rid of their garbage, a large percentage of which is recyclable Styrofoam. The cost in just disposal and landfill ($438,000) is staggering.

Waste Issues:

1. *Building more prisons to satisfy political agendas for getting tough on crime when crime statistics are going down.*

2. *Building private prisons that pay more attention to the corporate bottom line than to properly caring for inmates or effecting positive rehabilitation efforts.*

3. *Wasting tax dollars by providing inmates with substandard food that is discarded or stolen by officers.*

3

POLITICS & MEDIA HYPE BEHIND RUNAWAY PRISON GROWTH

Once criminal policy in the United States fell into the political arena, little could be done to recapture concern for limiting prison populations.

Alfred Blumstein
Carnegie-Mellon criminologist

Media hype and political rhetoric goes a great distance in molding public opinion about the prison system and prisoners. Inordinate attention to a criminal case—more than the 15 minutes of fame anyone deserves—reinforces the negative image of criminals. It also paints an unrealistic picture of the majority of the prison population that neither harbors hatred and anger at the whole world nor intends to maim and kill wantonly.

The National Criminal Justice Commission in 1995 confirmed this fact. "Although crime frequently soars to the top of the nation's list of major problems, those who follow public opinion have concluded that it is driven more by the media treatment of crime than by changes in crime rates."

Crime and punishment became an explosive issue in the late 1960s. We witnessed the protracted war in Vietnam. We saw racial riots erupt in our nation's urban areas from LA to Detroit. We watched college students take to the streets to protest war and injustice.

Politicians decided it was time to restore law and order across the land. Congress responded with major anti-crime legislation in 1968 that issued millions of dollars to local police and increased involvement of the federal government in local law enforcement.

The War on Drugs

Richard Nixon made crime and punishment a core campaign theme that year. Shortly after his election, he added narcotics to the list of America's leading enemies, and called for a national war on drugs. "The abuse of drugs has grown from essentially a local police problem into a serious national threat to the personal health and safety of millions of Americans," he declared. Big Brother was born.

About the same time, states began stripping sentencing flexibility from judges and parole boards. Bother liberals and conservatives called for mandatory minimum sentences for certain crimes. Liberals, because they thought the old system was fraught with racial discrimination, and conservatives, who argued that the system was excessively lenient.

When the war on drugs began, it cost about $110 million a year. By comparison, Bush's budget in fiscal year 2003 called for $19.2 billion to fight drugs. Yet drug trafficking and trade go on unabated. The years in between brought some of the toughest laws on the books.

Gary E. Johnson, Republican Governor of New Mexico, drew national attention early in his administration with his contention that the War on Drugs was a waste of taxpayer money. He approached the issue from a business point of view. "As a successful businessman, I believe that locking up more and more people who are non-violent drug offenders—people whose real problem is that they are addicted to drugs—is simply a waste of money and human resources."

Just as a business investment should be reviewed on the basis of its returns, Johnson notes so should a social policy be evaluated on its actual effectiveness. Using that as a standard, the War on Drugs is a failure.

"After 20-plus years of zero-tolerance policies and increasingly harsh criminal penalties, we have over a half million people behind bars on drug charges nationwide—more than the total prison population of all of Western Europe. We're spending billions of dollars to keep them locked up, yet the federal government's own research demonstrates that drugs are cheaper, purer, and more readily available than when this war was started. Heroin use is up. Ecstasy use is up. Teenagers say that marijuana is easier to get than alcohol. No matter how you slice it, this is no success story," Johnson reports.

In 1980, the federal government arrested a few hundred thousand people on drug charges. Today, we arrest 1.6 million people a year for drug offenses. Yet we still have a drug problem. What is the outer limit of this national policy, Johnson asks. $40 million and 3.2 million arrests a year? More? The costs clearly outweigh the benefits.

In New Mexico, the cost to the state of treating drug use as a crime is over $43 million per year—excluding local and federal expenditures, which would nearly triple that figure. Over half of that money goes to corrections costs. Yet, despite this outlay, New Mexico has one of the highest rates of drug-related crime and one of the highest heroin-usage rates in the nation. Clearly, money should be spent some other way.

Johnson points to a study by the RAND Corporation. It shows that every dollar spent on treatment instead of imprisonment saves $7 in state costs. Treatment is significantly more effective at reducing drug use than jail and prison. "The most cost-effective way to deal with nonviolent drug users would be to stop prosecuting them, and instead to make an effective spectrum of treatment services available to those who request it. If a person uses marijuana in his or her home, doing no harm to anyone other than arguably to himself or herself, that person, in my opinion, should not be arrested and issued a prison sentence."

Johnson argues that the government used the wrong criteria to measure success of its drug policies. They determine success "by whether drug use went up or down, or whether seizures went up or down or how many acres of coca we eradicated in South America. Instead of asking how many people smoked marijuana last year, we should ask if drug-related crime went up or down. Instead of asking how many people did heroin last year, we should ask whether heroin overdoses went up or down. We should ask if public nuisances associated with drug use and dealing went up or down. In sort, we should try to reduce the harm caused by and suffered by drug users, instead of simply trying to lock them all up."

Johnson advocates strong reform of our drug policies. "The goal should be to help those addicted to drugs to find a better way. The answer is not imprisonment and legal attack. The answer lies in sentencing reform, in supplying treatment on demand, and in delivering honest drug education to our kids. We need policies that reflect what we know about drug addiction rather than policies that seek to punish it.

"The days of a drug war waged against our people should come to an end. If we take a new approach—one that deals with drugs through a medical model rather than a criminal justice model—I guarantee that prison rates would drop, violent crime would decrease, property crime would decrease, overdose deaths would decrease, AIDS and hepatitis C would decrease, and more of those needing treatment for drug abuse would receive it."

Furthermore, Johnson believes that it we were to take these and other 'harm-reduction' approaches toward drug use, we would spend many times less than we currently spend on the drug war. "The benefit will be a society with less death, disease, crime, suffering, and imprisonment. Now, that's a sensible investment."

The system is corrupt. Drugs are prominent and easy to obtain. Thousands of police officers have been corrupted. Banks and other businesses have profited mightily from the money side of drugs. It's not the street dealer who's making the money. He still lives with his mother because he's barely making enough money to support himself.

We need to go after the big money behind drugs. We need to go after those who own the ships and airplanes that bring tons of marijuana, heroin, and cocaine into our country. And we have to go after corruption in our law enforcement system.

Get tough laws

Two different situations greatly influenced the rise of drugs and drug crimes that led to tougher sentencing laws. First, Vietnam veterans returned home after being exposed to a vast drug culture in Southeast Asia; many of them were addicted to hard drugs. Then there was organized crime that wanted the system to stay the way it was, even augment it, because it was a recruiting ground for the organization. They wanted to ensure that drugs proliferated rapidly and widely, giving them lucrative profits. Organized crime wanted officials to crack down on the little guys because they were cutting into their profit margin.

States across the country took their lead from the federal government and its passage of tough sentencing legislation. As federal laws became harsher and harsher, states like New York pioneered passage of very punitive sentencing laws.

In 1973, New York Governor Nelson Rockefeller set a new "get tough" standard by instilling mandatory 15-year prison terms for possessing small amounts of narcotics. The idea caught fire. Almost every state put enacted some form of mandatory sentencing legislation.

Throughout the 1980s, legislators competed with one another to establish harsher and harsher penalties. States like California ratcheted up their anti-drug efforts, deploying state helicopters to crack down on marijuana growers.

Although crime rates were falling, Reagan doubled the FBI budget, boosted spending on federal prisons, and expanded drug prosecutions. "Longer prison sentences and tougher treatments are beginning to pay dividends," he said. "And make no mistake: this is happening because you, the people, are fed up with crime. You're the ones who are organizing your local police, insisting that justice be carried out..."

A clear lesson emerged: crime paid. Bush Senior proved that in 1988, when he resurrected the ghost of paroled rapist Willie Horton to haunt Michael Dukakis until he dropped out of the presidential race. Bill Clinton went one further in 1992. He left the campaign trail to personally deny clemency to a mentally challenged man on death row in Arkansas.

Punishment had become a bi-partisan issue. In 1994, with crime on steady decline, Congress turned a blind—and greedy—eye and approved major anti-crime legislation, raising drug penalties and giving billions for more prisons and law enforcement agencies.

The current Bush Administration continues to push for more prisons. As governor of Texas, Bush Junior presided over a corrections system that locks up more residents at a higher rate than any other state, except

Louisiana. Bush's first budget proposal laid out more money for federal prisons to the tune of $1 billion.

Politicians will tell us the problem is crime, but what is the cause of most crimes? The most common myth that we are taught to believe is that the individual who committed a crime did it because they were evil or acting on evil temptations. This is entirely illogical. Prison officials and "get tough" politicians insult us by using this flimsy notion to scare us into accepting their strict policies. Sadly, the public goes along. Prisons keep criminals, like spooks, from scaring us in the dark.

Boogey man theory aside, the facts remain clear: Only 10-15 percent of inmates in the prison population is considered violent, true threats to society. They require continuous supervision. That means 85-90 percent of inmates are either non-violent offenders or inmates who repeat offenders. Most of their crimes were committed in the process of fighting a life of poverty and desperation.

Although child abusers, serial killers, and rapists represent a very small percentage of the prison population, politicians routinely use them to promote tough laws and build more prisons—at taxpayer expense. These types of offenders are generally housed in protective custody, because inmates in the general population would kill them. They are at the bottom of the social order, despised by other prisoners.

Many men and women in prison today were in the wrong place at the wrong time or, in a moment of weakness, committed a mistake that cost them years of freedom. They are not necessarily hard-hearted individuals or cold-blooded killers. They simply want to do their time and return to society.

Politics plays an enormous role in determining every aspect of the prison system, from sentencing criminals to building prisons to managing inmates in prison. Politics surely has played a major role in the Thomson prison fiasco. Originally, the prison was supposed to be built on a closed army depot. Its move to its present site shifted it from a Republican to a Democratic-controlled district.

The politics surrounding Thomson prison stand in the shadows of the state's financial woes. Add to that the increased spending by the current governor (without creating new revenue sources), and politics begin swimming in a sea of red ink that precludes opening this much-needed prison facility.

Three Strikes

In the early 1990s, the federal government and 23 states were passing "three-strikes" laws. Essentially that meant prison sentences of 25 years to life upon commission of a third felony. Although these laws have removed some violent offenders from our midst, they have also handed down life sentences to many thousands of people for petty crimes.

Legislators on both sides of the aisle voice concerns and offer solutions, none of which so far have taken hold and resolved the crisis that looms in the large prison system across the country. Especially at campaign time, we hear politicians wax tough on crime and cite statistics—real or manipulated—that justify tougher laws and longer sentences.

Despite strong voices from advocacy groups to the contrary, there still is a pervasive sentiment to 'lock ☒em up and throw away the keys'. Georgia has a 'two strikes' law; for sexual offenses, California allows only 'one strike.' Other states opt for humiliation: Arizona reinstated chain gangs. Such 'tough' reforms bring more votes at election time.

California, home of the 'three strikes' law, designed it to remove repeat violent offenders from society. The carrot that legislators used to get the bill passed quickly was the threat of brutal rapists and murderers preying on youngsters. But, those criminals continue to go about their business as usual. It is strange that the states with the strictest laws have the highest crime rate, such as California. So what has become of the 'three strikes' law?

It went from strictly targeting child abusers to locking up petty criminals. One was a boy caught stealing a pizza. It was his third arrest for stealing food. As a bounty hunter once related, "The boy was just hungry. They should have fed him, not imprisoned him for life." Yes, he received a three strikes life sentence, which, due to widespread public outcry, was eventually overturned and the young man was released.

Most people concur that punishment is warranted for crimes against society, but too much punishment can have an adverse effect. As prison systems practice more warehousing of men that degrades and humiliates them that discourages rehabilitative efforts of any kind, waste is the end result...enormous waste of our tax dollars and incalculable waste of human lives and potential.

Arizona was one of the first states to adopt the "truth in sentencing" laws, which require an offender to serve 85 percent of his sentence, thereby eliminating parole. The sentences there are harsher and longer than most other states. Arizona's prison population breaks down to 10 percent violent repeat offenders...the rest serving for nonviolent offenses and 77 percent of those are first-time offenders. Twenty-two percent of the prison population is serving time for non-violent drug possession. There must be a better way to manage drug possession convictions.

It is ironic that politicians call for more prisons and tougher prison laws to satisfy their need for instant gratification, when they should be doing everything to assure that their constituents' tax dollars are effectively spent. If they want to prevent crime, they should blaze new trails to check the root causes of street crime and support organizations that work to mitigate the social conditions that breed crime.

Crime rates fell dramatically in the 1990s, but a fierce debate continues as to what brought about the decline. Was it mass incarceration, as some politicians would have us believe? Not so quick.

In his bestseller, *Freakonomics*, Steven D. Levitt theorizes that *Roe v. Wade* has triggered the greatest crime-drop in recorded history. How so? Countless studies have shown that children born into an adverse environment are far more likely than other children are to become criminals.

Thanks to the millions of women who had abortions following passage of *Roe v. Wade*—most of them poor, unmarried, unemployed, and uneducated—millions of children were not born into the underbelly of society that would have eventually sucked them into a life of crime.

Media complicity

The media, especially cable and network television, have a vested interest in perpetuating crime. Crime stories sell. They boost ratings. With new competition from cable networks, 24-hour news channels,

TV news and programs about crime—dramatic, cheap to produce, and popular—have proliferated madly.

According to the Center for Media and Public Affairs, crime stories took first place on the nightly news over the past decade. From 1990 to 1998 homicide rates fell by half across the nation; yet homicide stories on the three major networks rose almost fourfold. Saturation coverage of that magnitude has a direct impact on the formation of public perceptions.

People perceived crime as a lingering problem, because they could not turn on their favorite TV news programs without seeing headlines about crimes. The grittier the crimes, the higher the ratings.

As a result, it has become "impossible to run an election campaign without advocating more jails, harsher punishment, more executions, all things that have never worked to reduce crime but have always worked to get votes," said George Gerbner, former dean of University of Pennsylvania's Annenberg School of Communication. "It's driven largely, although not exclusively, by television-cultivated insecurity."

In the next chapter, we address yet another nightmare—mandatory minimums—and examine the pros and cons of this harsh sentencing guideline that has unjustly trapped so many non-violent offenders in protracted sentences.

Waste Issues:

1. *Supporting legislation that incarcerates millions upon millions of non-violent drug offenders*

2. *Supporting legislation that protracts sentences far beyond a balanced crime/punishment ratio.*

3. *Allowing ourselves to let politicians and the media think for us and form our opinions*

4. *Turning a blind eye to big money and corruption behind the drug problem.*

4

Mandatory Minimums

*I have since come to realize that the
provisions of the [mandatory minimum
sentencing] law have led to terrible injustices
and that signing it was a mistake – an overly
punishing and cruel response that gave no
discretion to a sentencing judge, even for
extenuating circumstances.*

William G. Milliken
Former Michigan governor who originally
signed the mandatory minimum bill
into law in Michigan.

In the previous chapter, we examined the rise in drug use and the harsh sentencing laws that followed. The toughest laws were yet to come—those that ordered mandatory minimum sentencing.

With the explosion of the crack cocaine epidemic in the mid-1980s and the growing number of drug-related homicides, Congress looked to mandatory sentencing for drug-related crimes as a law enforcement weapon. The Anti-Drug Abuse Act of 1986 established federal mandatory minimum sentencing guidelines.

Under the law, judges were forced to impose fixed sentences on offenders convicted of a crime, regardless of culpability or other mitigating circumstances. Before the 1986 law, drug offenders received an average prison sentence of 22 months. After the law was enacted, the average sentenced jumped to 66 months.

"I remember that there was increasing concern on my part and around the state on the growing drug traffic," recalls former Michigan Governor William G. Milliken. "I signed the mandatory minimum bill into law near the end of my governorship. It had to do with penalties for possession of 650 grams or more of hard drugs. We were trying to catch the kingpins, but instead we got a lot of little guys, some of whom were addicts who were trying to supply their habit. Very few were involved in drug trafficking. We did not foresee the problems that these laws would create."

The new laws not only failed, but also they created a new crisis. Unfair sentences negatively affect the offenders' families and impact the city and county jails that hold offenders too long in dreadfully overcrowded states because judges do not have the discretion to set lower sentences.

Traditionally, judges weighed all the facts of a case before determining an appropriate sentence. But, with enactment in many states of mandatory minimum laws, judges are left with little wiggle room. Predetermined sentences are handed down automatically to those found guilty.

"With the power of release taken away from parole authorities, and judge's discretion also removed, it was left by default to the legislatures to set sentencing policy," said Franklin Zimring, a criminologist at the University of California at Berkley.

Legislators touted harsh, inflexible sentencing as a way to nab the big-time dealers of the drug trade and as a deterrent for others farther down the line. Police and prosecutors were quick to use the threat of a long sentence with low-level drug dealers or to promote snitching among them against drug kingpins. It hasn't worked that way. Instead, our prisons have been filled to capacity and beyond with low-level offenders at a higher price tag for taxpayers.

Under the mandatory sentencing guidelines, the power to choose the most appropriate sentence for the crime shifted to prosecutors. They decided the charges and controlled the plea bargains. They usually picked long prison terms as plea bargains, because the offender, who often faced multiple, excessive charges, got even more years under the mandatory sentencing guidelines. Particularly in drug and alcohol cases, the system went gone totally out of control. Far too many people went to prison that would have been helped better by drug treatment programs and intensive probation.

After reviewing a growing body of evidence and working with a number of prisoners, Governor Milliken concluded that signing mandatory minimum sentencing into law in Michigan was a mistake. "As I got into it deeper and deeper, I increasingly felt that it was a harsh and unjust law. I have worked ever since on getting the law amended, and continue to do so. Taking discretion away from the judges was a very unfortunate mistake."

Along with passage of this law to increase lengths of prison terms, the number of inmates incarcerated for drug-related crimes increased. The prison population grew so quickly that prisons soon became overcrowded, which increased the costs to the prison system as more corrections officers and prisons were needed to effectively manage the growing population.

Most of the growth in prison population has been for nonviolent offenders; especially those convicted on drug charges. Due to mandatory sentencing laws, over half of today's inmates are incarcerated on drug charges, despite evidence that treatment programs are much more effective at preventing future drug offenses.

Now, 20 years after passage of mandatory minimum sentences, the laws have failed to deter drug dealers or users. Drugs, in fact, are cheaper, purer, and more plentiful than ever before.

It is obvious that the system has failed. The criminal justice system has been so distorted; even the U. S. Supreme Court cannot fix it. The judge's traditional role has been diminished, given way to enhanced power of the prosecutor. The result has been less fairness and a prison population growing out of control.

Judges have been in the best position to observe how corrosively the war on drugs has affected our legal system by overwhelming the court dockets with non-violent offenders, by eroding civil liberties, and imposing disproportionate penalties under mandatory minimum sentencing law.

Not so long into working with the new guidelines, judges became the most vocal critics of mandatory minimums and of the war on drugs itself. Judges Against the Drug War, an online database of judicial opinions, is critical of the war on drugs and the sentencing laws imposed on judges at the loss of their discretion.

A growing number of judges have become bitter over the change in their roles in sentencing. As one judge said, "The people who drew up these guidelines never sat in a court and had to look a defendant in the eye while imposing some of these sentences."

Even former U.S. Supreme Court Justice William Rehnquist thought these laws had more to do with politics than criminology. "Mandatory Minimums are frequently the result of floor amendments to demonstrate emphatically that legislators want 'to get tough on crime.'"

Other judges are speaking out.

Senior Circuit Judge Myron H. Bright of the 8th Circuit Court in 1993 cited the case of a man with a child-mind that received 30 years of incarceration. "In this case, the lowest person on the totem pole, a mere street-level seller with an IQ of 53, received a heavier sentence than the mastermind of the conspiracy, and the conspiracy's primary drug supplier. What kind of system would produce such a result? This case provides yet another example of how rigid sentencing guidelines and the mandatory minimums associated with drug cases make an unfair 'criminal' system."

In another case, Judge Bright wrote, "Unwise sentencing policies, which put men and women in prison for years, not only ruin lives, but also drain the American taxpayers. It is time to call a halt to the unnecessary and expensive cost of putting people in prison for a long time based on the mistaken notion that such an effort will win The War on Drugs. The public needs to know that unnecessary, harsh and unreasonable drug sentences serve to waste billions of dollars without doing much good for society. We have an unreasonable system."

From a political standpoint, mandatory minimums are very popular. They satisfy the public desire to get tough on crime. "If you do the crime, you do the time."

From a human—and from an enlightened intellectual—standpoint, these laws are totally absurd: each case is different. For non-violent drug crimes, incarceration doesn't even make sense. If we're an enlightened people, drug and alcohol abusers should be in a treatment facility, not a prison, which is what we're doing now.

Finally, in 2004, Governor Blagojevich opened a drug prison in Illinois. After a person is convicted and sentenced, he goes to Joliet to the processing center for all the prisons to determine where he will serve his time. If he is certifiably criminally insane, he goes to the facility at Chester. Or, if he is a sex offender, he is assigned to a special facility in Joliet.

Faced with a growing drug problem, the state re-opened the Sheridan facility and launched the Sheridan (IL) National Model Drug Prison Reentry Program. This program—the first of its kind in Illinois—offers intensive drug treatment to all inmates (drug addicts) at the facility and a job preparedness program. The recidivism rate among Sheridan inmates is down by 50 percent.

Then, in recognition of the rapid rise in the use of methamphetamine, the governor, in his 2006 State of the State address, proposed creation of a specialized prison and treatment facility (at the 667-bed Southwestern Illinois Correction Center) for meth addicts, patterned after the Sheridan program.

More than 12 million Americans have tried meth and 1.5 million are regular users. In Illinois, the number of meth labs dismantled grew from 24 in 1997 to 961 in 2004. Illinois laws regulating meth are the toughest in the nation.

The impact of inflexibility

In 2000, the Uniform Crime Reports indicated that states with neither "three strikes" laws nor truth-in-sentencing guidelines had the lowest rates of index crimes. States with both types of get tough laws, on the other hand, had the highest index crime rates.

By 2002, the country's jail and prison population had swelled to over two million for the first time in history. Prison overcrowding and strained state and local budgets have resulted.

In the report from the National Institute of Justice published that same year, their findings showed that "get tough on crime" approaches have zero measurable impact on overall drug violence, as perpetrated by gangs. Due to the prevalence of gang violence largely in urban ghettos and the federal government's determination to control the problem, Congress passed new legislation in 2005 that defines gang size. [Another example of Big Brother's involvement in social issues, which our founding fathers did not intend.] The Gang Deterrence and Community Protection Act defines a gang as having as few as three members, making it sufficient to be called a federal case. The Act calls for stiff mandatory minimum sentences for gang-related crimes and puts tens of millions of dollars towards prisons. The NIJ report shows conclusively that exaggerated jail terms have no deterrent effect at all.

For gangs, the only responses found to be successful were the "life skills" programs advocated by authorities like Los Angeles Sheriff Lee Baca, such as teaching conflict resolution and positive self-esteem. Intervention programs, like Ceasefire, which scored high success rates in Boston and several other major cities by curtailing gang activity, was the only strategy singled out in the entire report as having caused a substantial reduction in youth homicide. Yet officials seem unimpressed.

David Kennedy, criminologist and architect of Operation Ceasefire, blames the fact that most people adopt one of two very different responses to crime: the *criminal justice response*, which is all about the moral responsibility of individuals and the belief that tougher enforcement can influence those individuals. And the *root-cause approach*, which emphasizes the role of racism and economic inequality in crime.

The problem, according to Kennedy, is that neither approach defines an effective crime-control strategy. "The biggest problem lies with the dysfunctional nature of American law enforcement. Comparing criminal justice to a real profession, like medicine", he points out that in criminal justice there is no real professionalism. How do you get to be a judge? Get a law degree. How do you get to be a DA? Get elected. There is no collective knowledge, no relationship between theory and practice.

"There was a time when surgeons were barbers, and what medicine did was bootstrap itself up. In criminal justice, we're still barbers, and if people in these communities, paying the tax bills and burying their kids and visiting their raped daughters in intensive care, knew the way business was conducted, there would be bodies hanging from oak trees. The presumption that most people have, that this is serious, thoughtful work, and that if you don't get good results it's because absolutely nothing works, is so wrong."

Advocacy groups, like Families Against Mandatory Minimums (FAMM), whose membership includes everyone from judges to inmates, challenge inflexible, excessive penalties. Their strongest argument is that the punishment must fit the crime.

FAMM promotes sentencing policies that give judges discretionary power to distinguish between defendants and sentence them to their role in the offense, the seriousness of the offense, and the potential for their rehabilitation.

"Mandatory sentences are counterproductive. They are more harmful to the community than helpful, they're a big waste of money," said Jeff Stewart, member of FAMM.

It is not economically feasible to spend money on incarceration of any form, let alone mandatory minimums, in drug areas. The result is a failed social policy that has given us undue incarceration and inadequate drug treatment. It is time to re-examine this issue.

Turning the corner

The result of 'get tough' decisions filled our prisons with large numbers of non-violent and drug offenders at exorbitant costs to the taxpayers, and yet increasing evidence abounds that mass incarceration does little, if anything, to achieve public safety.

Some of the toughest drug penalties in the country have been passed by legislatures in Michigan and New York. However, in 1998, Michigan overturned its notorious "650-lifer law" that mandated life in prison without parole for offenders convicted of intent to deliver 650 grams or more of heroin or cocaine.

Prison costs and crowding are forcing other states to reconsider mandatory drug sentencing. Louisiana has dropped mandatory sentencing for a wide variety of non-violent offenses, including drugs. Indiana eliminated mandatory 20-year sentences for cocaine sales.

Connecticut granted judges limited discretion in sentencing non-violent drug offenders.

In December 2002, the Michigan Senate passed a historic package of three sentencing reform bills that eliminate most of the state's mandatory minimum sentences for drug offenses. The reform allows judges to impose sentences based on a range of factors in each case, rather than solely on drug weight and type. It also restores judges' discretion to "fit the punishment to the crime" and replaces lifetime probation for the lowest-level offenders with a five-year probationary period. Furthermore, it allows judges to impose consecutive sentences for delivery offenses but not for possession offenses. It also permits earlier parole eligibility for some prisoners serving "under 650" mandatory minimum and mandatory consecutive drug sentences at the discretion of the parole board.

Rep. Bill McConico, a Detroit Democrat who sponsored the bill, said the legislation is a major step that brings fairness back to the judicial system in Michigan. "The overwhelming bipartisan support for this legislation shows it is not a partisan issue. We were able to unite Republicans, Democrats, prosecutors, judges, and families in a common cause of sentencing justice. Now we can reunite families, reallocate resources, and allow judges to do their job." Republican Governor John Engler signed the bill into law.

Executive Director Laura Sager of FAMM applauded Michigan lawmakers for taking "a principled stand on this important issue. This vote restores confidence in the fairness of the criminal justice system. Harsh mandatory minimums, originally intended to target drug kingpins, have instead warehoused many non-violent, low-level drug offenders at a very high cost to taxpayers."

David Morse, president of the Prosecuting Attorneys Association of Michigan, shared that organization's support of the legislation. "Michigan's prosecutors recognize that an effective drug policy is a combination of criminal justice strategies, readily available drug treatment programs, incarceration where appropriate, and prevention activities in schools, businesses, and homes. That is why we support a responsible approach to replacing the mandatory minimum sentences for drug crimes with sentences that are appropriate for the crime."

The legislation is consistent with principles supported by many organizations, including judicial discretion and cost-effective and flexible sentencing guidelines. They are also part of the solution to Michigan's skyrocketing corrections cost.

People in former get-tough-on-crime states like Illinois no longer consider public safety a priority concern. They have replaced it with growing concerns over education and employment, issues that hit home more directly with a larger percentage of the population.

Politicians in coming elections in Illinois, therefore, are not expected to make crime a campaign issue, unlike previous campaign years.

"What today's politician needs to say," explains Morgan Moss, director of the Center for Therapeutic Justice in Williamsburg, Virginia, "is I'm tougher than my opponent on crime, but my approach to toughness is different. His way has been shown to be a dismal failure, and I can back that up with statistics. My approach works, and I can show that beyond a shadow of a doubt. We're going to be smart on crime, not tough on crime, but in the long run it's going to be tougher on crime than get-tough on crime is."

Waste Issues:

1. *Removing discretion from judges, forcing them to hand down sentences without considering mitigating circumstances*

2. *Perpetuating tough legislation for non-violent and drug offenders*

3. *Misusing taxpayer dollars to house and care for offenders given unwarranted sentences.*

4. *Wasting human lives and potential through unfair and inappropriate sentences.*

5

HOUSTON, WE HAVE A PROBLEM

A thousand men loaded with error
cannot withstand one man
armed with the truth.

Anonymous

The critical problem in our criminal justice system is that we have created such a negative culture that when people move into that culture and become acclimated to that culture, they become hypnotized by it. After a bit, they know better how to function in that environment than they do on the outside.

That was apparent in the Hoover Commission Report of 2003. In California, where there are 160,000 people in their prison system, that pool of people was almost a natural resource. They were tending that natural resource, not intentionally, but the unintended consequence was that they were protecting that natural resource for fear of losing it.

In California, one of the most important issues is the union that represents the corrections officers. They are afraid of losing their jobs. That union is one of the most influential and powerful lobbies in the state. If someone went to the governor with a foolproof way to reduce the prison population there by 10 percent a year, the governor would be skeptical, but when offered a guarantee, he would agree to try it. However, as soon as he would get ready to implement that plan, he would find himself running headlong into all kinds of opposition and obstacles, because they would see it as losing jobs.

Three powerful things—economics, politics, and the media—keep the system entrenched where it is. The fourth element is the people. They get so acclimated; it would take a radical shift for them that by and large they would not consider it. That's what we're up against.

Sure, you can save dollars along the way, but the answer is not in spending more money on programs. The answer is in changing the culture of incarceration itself. Enter any jail or prison and you will see a culture of control, intimidation, and power.

The Abu Ghraib prison problem in Iraq was not a strange aberration. It was simply a transplant of how we treat prisoners here in America. That's all it was, even the people who were doing it. The head of the prison system there came from the prison system in Virginia. The same things we did in Iraq—and Guantanamo—go on in our maximum-security prisons here.

The culture is deeply engrained in the people who work in it. It is deeply engrained in the people who fill the cells. It is deeply engrained in the politicians and law enforcement officers.

The only thing that will make a difference is changing the culture. That will take a paradigm shift. But when you talk about that, people go to the worst case scenario. Politicians and the media say, oh, you mean coddling inmates. This isn't about coddling.

This is about not having forced idleness, which is one of the worst situations that you can put human beings in. "If you were to put me in a cell and tell me I had to stare at the same cinderblock for 23 hours a day, seven days a week for the rest of my life, I'd go insane," says Morgan Moss. "Animals in the zoo that are used to being free with their lives in balance, get put in a cage where they have everything natural taken away from them. Confine human beings to a cage and they will act in predictable ways."

In our jails and prisons, we confine men and women to cages and treat them like they are incompetent, incapable, unworthy, and believe that our job is to make their lives miserable. That's the culture of a negative environment. That's the prison system we have now.

The Hoover Commission Report determined that California should decide who were the really dangerous criminals that posed a threat to society. Those people you have to keep away from society at almost any cost.

But those dangerous people equal a maximum of 10 percent of those locked up. We're treating 90 percent the way 10 percent should be treated. When you do that to the 90 percent, you further marginalize them. The revolving door people are 95-98 percent drug addicts and alcoholics. Unless they receive services to check their addictions, they're never going to stop coming and going, particularly when the system focuses more on locking up low-level offenders than on locking up serious criminals.

We must address the needs of these people. We have to turn it around. If you simply start treating them with dignity and respect, as capable people, allowing them with a little support to form a network within the institution, then remarkable things start to happen. They stop acting like caged animals. They are no longer destructive of property or harmful to themselves and others. The suicide attempt rate goes to almost zero. The violence goes to almost zero—violence to themselves, to other inmates, and to the prison staff.

All of a sudden, the culture of that facility has done a 180. The Center for Effective Justice in Virginia, under the direction of Morgan Moss, has seen this happen time and again in jails there. "It works beyond a shadow of a doubt. The same would work in prisons, too. In our community models in jails, the security staff has almost nothing to do. There is no forced idleness, because inmates are busy in a volunteer, self-selected program from 7 AM to 7 PM. Very little cost is involved, save for a few supplies and a supervisor. In these program pods, you do not see the robotic walks and talks that are the common denominator of jails and prisons across the country."

Moss and his staff emphasize programs in jails over prisons. "When you introduce this program in jails, you intervene and keep large numbers of people from doing decades in prison. In a few months to a year in jail, they can make real progress."

Another major area neglected in every penal institution is the visit. If you have a family member in prison and you go to visit that person, normally you are going to be treated like dirt. You may well be abused. You will be treated like a third class citizen or worse.

Visits are important to jails and prisons for the management of inmates. As a warden or superintendent, one of the best things I can do to keep my facility under control is to treat visiting families and friends with respect. Honor them when they come to visit; inmates maintaining family ties, valuing them, and getting the support of that network are easier to manage than those who are cut off. This is not rocket science. This is basic human nature, common sense.

While people are on the inside, give them something constructive to do instead of existing on forced idleness. Address issues such as addiction, anger, domestic violence, parenting, relationships, and communication.

"One of the first men I worked with in a jail a few years ago," Moss recalls, "was transferred to a prison. In jail, he had been one of the most positive people in the program. After a while he wrote to me. 'I thought I would start a small support group. So some other positive guys and I would get together and talk. We decided to start a 12-step support group.'

"They hauled him into the warden's office, and the warden asked, 'What the hell do you think you're doing?' The prisoner responded, 'We have a group, and we support each other as we try to work on our issues of addiction and so on.'

"The warden yelled, 'I want to tell you something. There have been no goddamned A-A meetings in this prison since I've been here, and as long as I'm here there won't be none of that shit here. Get back to your cell and don't let me ever hear of you doing that again.'"

Stories like this one can be duplicated in prisons across the country. When you treat prisoners as human beings deserving of dignity and respect, people change. The only ones that don't change are those so damaged, so institutionalized, so mentally ill or so anti-social, they are incapable of changing. Everybody else changes.

For a small percentage of people working in jails and prisons, treating inmates with dignity and respect is directly contrary to their world view of inmates being lower than dirt, the view that it is their job to abuse inmates and feel powerful when they are abusing them. If someone starts showing them that inmates should not be treated that way and that they will rise up when they are not treated that way, such prison personnel will feel their views are threatened.

Another thing that happens when enlightened programs like this are implemented in jails and prisons: the percentage of people coming back changes dramatically. Instead of a 67 percent failure rate, the institution has a 67 percent success rate. If only 10 percent of the people who normally would return to prison don't—do the math. How many tens of millions of taxpayer dollars would be saved?

Most of these in-and-out prisoners are addicts. An addict on the street drinking and drugging commits, on average, 25 crimes a week. Again, do the math. How many crimes would be reduced a week if just 10 percent now have a job, pay taxes, do not commit crimes, and do not end up as indigents in the emergency room several times a month on overdosing with no way to pay for it?

The prison problem is systemic. We need the enlightened drug court approach. We need effective probation and parole supervision, not the old "if you don't go straight I'm going to lock you up again" approach. That approach is totally worthless, counter-productive, and wastefully expensive.

We need to lock people up as a last resort. While they are in prison, use the environment as human service centers and help inmates make the most of their time. When they are released, have their families ready to receive them and have them educated, too. Have probation or parole ready to offer positive intervention.

If this system were approached across the country, within five years we would totally change the culture of the criminal justice system in America. But doing the same thing over and over again and expecting different results has never worked. We can show that this approach works. The next decade of locking people up for $25,000 a year or a quarter of a million for a 10-year sentence is a total waste.

The result for the criminal justice system would be a safe and orderly operation of each facility. The staff would no longer have feces thrown at them. They wouldn't be knifed in the hallway. The facility would not be torn to shreds on a regular basis. Litigation costs would plummet, because people would not sue or attempt to commit suicide.

The retention of corrections staff would increase, because they are going to feel better about their own safety, be less stressful and confident that they have made a positive contribution by the end of their shift. The high rates of turnover, violence, destruction, and suicide would go down. And everyone would keep their jobs. We would save tax dollars and increase public safety and we would turn lives around across the board.

Waste issues:

1)   *Spending too many tax dollars on ineffective programs*

2)   *Putting prisoners in forced idle situations for extended periods of time*

6

RACIAL DISPARITIES

*If you are born poor and black in America,
you have a greater chance of going
to prison than you have receiving
proper healthcare or education.*

Marian Wright Edelman

Martin Luther King, Jr. would be furious. Despite positive strides to eliminate prejudice, we have not become color blind in America. In fact, we are far from it. We disenfranchise people of color in the election process, and Florida in 2000 was a good example of that. We keep minorities poor and deny them justice. We perpetuate the racial divide in our communities and institutions.

Nowhere is the racial divide more evident than in our prisons. We flooded the streets of urban ghettos with crack cocaine, a cheaper version of powder cocaine. Because crack is more affordable for poor minorities, it became a tool of law enforcement to justify the mass incarceration of black men. Despite the fact that more whites than blacks actually use crack, 88 percent of prison sentences for crack offenses go to blacks.

The infamous '100 to 1' rule came on the heels of crack introduction into our cities. The rule, which means that a person can be in possession of 100 times more powder cocaine than crack to get a mandatory sentence, targeted minorities.

Statistics bear these facts out. In 1926, whites comprised 79percent of inmates entering state and federal prisons; blacks made up 21 percent. The Washington, DC-based Sentencing Project found in 1990 that on, on average, one in every four black men from 20 to 29 years of age were either in some form of custody (jail, probation, prison or parole).

Stringent sentencing laws unfairly targeted poor people of color in the 1980s and 1990s. Sentences handed down put them behind bars for longer periods of time than ever before.

In 1996, Human Rights Watch reported that blacks constituted a staggering 90 percent of all drug offenders admitted to prison in Illinois. By 2000, the percentage had barely fallen to 89 percent; ranking Illinois number two in racial disparity in its state prisons.

By the turn of the century (1999), African American men represented 55 percent of the prison population, and 60 percent of all new admissions to state and federal prisons.

The racial disparities are incredible across the country. America is home to more than 2 million prisoners and roughly half of them are black, even though African Americans make up less than 13 percent of the nation's population. One in 10 prisoners in the *world* is an African American male. According to the Justice Policy Institute, there are now more black men behind bars than in college in the United States.

The racial composition of the ex-offender population is striking. According to the latest social science estimates from Christopher Uggen of the University of Minnesota and Jeff Maza at Northwestern, nearly one in five black men in the U.S. has a prison record and a staggering one in three black men now possess a felony record.

Within three years of release from prison, 40 percent of the nation's ex-prisoners cycles back to prison. The modern American mass incarceration state is fed by recycling disadvantaged ex-offenders back into the prison system. Of the more than 730,000 people entering prison or jail each year, 33 percent have been there before.

According the Bureau of Justice Statistics, based on current rates of incarceration, an estimated 32 percent of black males will enter prison during their lifetime, compared with 17 percent of Hispanic males and 5.9 percent of white males.

Being arrested and incarcerated almost brings a badge of honor for young minority men. Avoiding a criminal record is considered a stroke of good luck.

Once released from prison, many prisoners face a grim existence due to a lack job skills and employer suspicion. In most states, convicted felons are not allowed to vote from prison; in 12 states, felons are disenfranchised for life. These factors contribute to widespread unemployment in minority communities as well as meager election representation.

Prison time serves "to channel individuals away from skilled occupations and into job sectors which are characterized by low wages, limited job stability, and fewer opportunities for advancement," notes sociologist Devah Pager. "Overall, incarceration appears to disrupt the career-building process such that prior work experience contributes little to future opportunities. Ex-offenders are left to start back at square one with respect to gaining a foothold in a particular occupation."

One story sums up the problem of black minorities in America. A California prisoner, years ago, worked toward a Ph.D. from a local university. For his thesis, he wrote, "The poor minorities of this country basically have no way to contribute to the capitalistic society we have and the economics of America. Their way of contributing, therefore, is to be the fodder for the gristmill of the prison industrial complex. They are the natural resource. That is the way they contribute and without that natural resource, the system would not be able to function." A disgusting, repulsive thought, but nonetheless true.

Illinois

As of June 2001, there were nearly 20,000 more black males in Illinois state prisons than the number of black males enrolled in the state's public universities. There were more black males in the state's correctional facilities on drug charges alone than the total number of black males enrolled as undergraduates in state universities. Just 992 black males received bachelor's degrees (3.3 of all conferred) from those universities in 1999. Seven thousand black males were released from the Illinois state prison system in 2000 just for drug offenses.

In 2003 Illinois, a state with only a 15 percent black population, has a prison population that is two thirds black. Two years earlier, the state's incarceration rate for African Americans was more than ten times the rate for whites.

To house its growing number of disproportionately black and urban-based prisoners, the state built 20 adult prisons, an average of one a year, beginning in 1980. Mass incarceration was one of the leading growth items in the state's budget in the last 16 years, increasing from just over a third the amount it spends on higher education to nearly three fourths.

Two years ago, in Illinois, it cost almost $21,000 to house an adult prisoner and more than $50,000 to incarcerate a juvenile. The cost of incarcerating one adult is equal to more than four and a half times the state's legally mandated public education 'foundation level' of $4,5460—the minimum expenditure determined to be required to meet the educational needs of a single child.

The prison construction boom—fed by the rising "market" of black offenders—provides an extraordinary source of jobs, tax dollars, and associated local economic multipliers for downstate Illinois communities.

Conservatively speaking, each prisoner is worth $25,000 of local economic development each year. Mass incarceration transfers as much as a billion dollars each year from the state's mostly Chicago-based black community to the state's predominantly white and rural prison towns.

Those towns and the correctional unions that represent their prison workers (AFSCME Council 31 in Illinois, which lobbied for the construction of the state's inhumane "Supermax" facility in the town of Tamms—have joined hands with prison-contracting corporations and 'law and order' politicians. Together they work for a politically powerful prison industrial complex that pushes incarceration as an economic development program regardless of mass imprisonment's impact on public safety.

In Illinois and the entire nation, mass incarceration is a civil rights problem, period. It exacerbates the social, political, and economic disenfranchisement of inner city black communities and deepens the divide of wealth and income between blacks and whites.

Disproportionately criminalizing and incarcerating poor black men in Illinois and elsewhere perpetuates segregation and inequality that led them into crime in the first place. It deepens the disadvantage in the labor market for hundreds of thousands of minority men and women. In addition to the stigma of poverty and disadvantage, incarceration gives blacks a new stigma, a criminal record and the trauma of incarceration that lingers throughout their lives.

After release, it removes potential wage, purchasing power, economic development, and political clout from the minority communities and businesses. It works against key policy goals of the larger community: public safety, stable family foundation, long-term labor market involvement, poverty reduction, equal opportunity, racial integration, harmony, balanced community development, civic engagement, and education.

These numbers and disparities are not unique to Illinois. Thanks to a 30-year campaign of racially disparate surveillance, arrest, sentencing, and incarceration carried out under the auspices of the war on drugs, things have reached the point where no nation has ever imprisoned a higher percentage of its people than the contemporary United States. We are home to 6 percent of the world's people and 25 percent of its prisoners.

Wealth

America is the wealthiest nation on earth, but we cannot provide education for all of our children. We cannot provide health care for all of our citizens; more than 40 million are without basic health insurance. We cannot match unemployment benefits to the growing numbers of those without jobs. We lack or claim to lack sufficient funds to rehabilitate or provide re-entry services to millions of disproportionately black prisoners and ex-prisoners that will always live under the shadow of a criminal record. What then are we doing with all the money that gives us the title of the world's wealthiest nation?

We spend trillions of dollars on tax cuts for the top 1 percent of the population and billions on the military many times over than all of our enemy states combined. We provide massive subsidies to high-tech corporations for weapons and anti-terrorist defense systems when there is no legitimate threat to the American people. We imprison more people and spend more money on incarceration that any nation in history. We spend billions of dollars invading other countries, while cutting back dramatically on services for our own people.

Waste Issues:

1.   *Failing to address the root causes of crime in minority communities*

2.   *Sentencing minorities disproportionately to prison*

7

CLEAR & PRESENT DANGER

All natural tendencies toward stability
appear to have evaporated. Not only has
there been a quantum leap of
unprecedented proportions in prison
populations, but there appear also to be
no indications of any counter forces which
might impose limits.

Andrew Rutherford
British criminologist

In previous chapters, we have examined the criminal justice system from the standpoints of excessive incarceration through tough sentencing laws and disproportionate sentencing of minorities. Now, the obvious result of too much incarceration is overcrowding. One might assume that happens just in third world countries. Some countries, in fact, more closely resemble gulags than our prisons do. In one African jail, for instance, the feet of prisoners rot off because there is standing room only and men must stand in their own waste for days and weeks on end. Prisoners there might consider our prisons hotels by comparison.

Housing more inmates in a cell that what it is designed for is common in the United States and, in fact, is becoming more common with people serving longer sentences, adding to the population problem.

In state prisons, on average, inmates are male, around 30 years of age, and high school dropouts (only 22 percent finished high school and 50-75 percent cannot read).

More than 50 percent (and as many as 70 percent in some states) of prison inmates are repeat offenders, at least twice for violent crimes. Most of them held jobs prior to their arrest, but their income reflected the problem that drives many men into a life of crime. They earned less than $10,000 a year. Almost half of them admitted that another family member was incarcerated at the same time.

A prison is a society within a society with its own gangs, rules, laws, politics, courts, and even their own prisons inside prisons (Security Housing Units or SHU). Prisons mirror many of the problems in a free society—jobs, unemployment, barriers, riots, wars, treaties, and truces. Of course, crime is ever present.

In cell houses of a hundred or more inmates living in warehousing conditions, things can get a little dicey. Corrections officers, on first blush, appear to have control, but basically they contain, ensure they don't get hurt and no one escapes. Many officers have less education than some of their charges and a growing number of them have no cognitive skills that help them effectively relate to people of other races and cultures.

In Indiana, for instance, it is mandatory now for newly hired officers to have a high school education or GED equivalent. That was not always true, and today it still is not always true. Most prisons in rural areas allow prison officials to do the hiring. Nepotism, as we have said earlier, is readily practiced. Joe Doe submits his application and says he graduated from South Side High School, but everyone knows he didn't complete the fourth grade. Besides, his Aunt Sally has worked at the prison for years. No one checks these applications, so many unqualified prison workers slip through the cracks.

The biggest problem is that the current wage scale does not attract the people who have an education and high economic standards. When states build in rural areas, they need to offer wages that will bring highly qualified people from urban centers to less than exciting rural areas.

One would think that in institutions where security is the number one priority, one would not find more crime there than in the high crime areas outside. It's much easier to buy drugs in prison than on the street, although the cost is higher because the middleman [the officer] has to get paid. Officers have their own drug turf, and inmates are killed in drug wars between territories. Even officers have gone into the tobacco business where prisons have outlawed smoking.

In maximum-security prisons—or more likely in them—there is prostitution, bribery, murder, rape, and extortion. Rape is commonplace. And with more female officers insisting on equality inside male populated prisons, the incidence of sexual misconduct has risen dramatically. The same is true where men oversee female prisoners.

Overcrowded prisons are rife with disease, physical abuse, and danger. Inmates face exposure to deadly diseases through forced or voluntary sex, intravenous drug use or sharing cells with infected fellow convicts. Considering the fact that most prisoners return to their communities, bringing these diseases with them, should alarm us. An outbreak of meningitis in LA's city jail spread into nearby neighborhoods in the early 1990s.

In most prisons where healthcare is minimal at best, not much is done to track illnesses like HIV, hepatitis C, and tuberculosis. Even less is done to prevent the spread of those diseases. As a result no one knows the exact extent of the problem, but virtually all the evidence indicates that the U.S. penal system is a prime breeding ground for some of the world's deadliest diseases, ultimately hastening their spread beyond prison walls.

In 2000, John Miles, director of the federal Centers for Disease Control and Prevention, told a large group of prison doctors and nurses that more than 600,000 inmates are released every year—and many of them are riddled with disease. According to the Bureau of Justice Statistics, 24,000 inmates nationwide were HIV positive in 1996. Just five years later, in 2001, the number had almost doubled, spreading 10 times faster than in the general population. TB, a highly contagious lung disease, infects 1 in 4 people in some prisons, compared to fewer than 1 in 10,000 in the general population.

Hepatitis C, an often-lethal liver disease spread by blood exchange, infects an estimated 41 percent of inmates in California prisons alone, compared to less than 2percent in the general population.

Miles calls prisons "the nation's reservoir of disease", but he feels, like many officials, that inmates bring their diseases with them from the outside—a side effect of drug use and risky sexual practices many of them indulged in before being locked up.

On the downside and contributing to a lot of the uncertainty about the spread and incubation of some of these diseases is the fact that the Center for Disease Control (CDC) has failed to conduct any study that might show how prison life spreads disease.

"The CDC does not want to know the truth," says Cal Skinner, a former state representative in Illinois. He wanted to know if prisons were "handing down unadjudicated death sentences" by breeding AIDS and then spreading the disease outside prison. When Skinner could not come up with any answers to his question, he petitioned for documents under the Freedom of Information Act. He eventually uncovered a 1990 study by the CDC, which spent $483,000 tracking the rate of new infections in Illinois jails. The study found that 3 out of every 1,000 inmates catch HIV in jail each year—more than 10 times the statewide rate.

The results were never published, although the CDC validated accuracy of the study, despite their claims of faulty blood samples, which caused the CDC to withhold publication. Skinner wondered if it was important enough to spend almost half a million dollars on the study and the study was faulty why has the CDC not conducted another study?

For the most part, the CDC and other public health agencies have limited themselves to tracking current levels of disease among prisoners, while avoiding studies of new infection rates.

Whatever the health problems, overcrowded prisons provoke them. More drugs, more needle sharing. More double and triple bunking. More opportunities for unwanted or wanted sex. Cell houses jammed to capacity and beyond, more people sharing the same stagnant air.

Studies in various states over the years have shown that 14 percent of inmates were forced into sex. In one survey 87 percent of Texas prison officials claimed that rape was a common occurrence, but inmate testimonies reveal that officials look the other way rather than deal with the problem head-on. Some prisons have a 1 in 10 rate of forcible rape, often by repeated gang rape. The bottom line estimate in 2001 by Stop Prison Rape, a California-based advocacy group, is that as many as 364,000 prisoners are raped every year.

There are fewer studies available to track the problem of needle sharing. Inmates openly admit the ease of obtaining drugs inside prison (with officer complicity). One Tennessee study found that 28 percent of inmates shoot up behind bars.

TB lately has drawn considerable attention because it can spread so easily from prisons to the general public, through visits in the prison, interaction with prison staff and prisoners, and when prisoners are released back to their communities. In the 1990s, a deadly strain of TB swept through the New York state prison system, infecting 39 prisoners and two correction officers, one who died, along with 35 prisoners. As a result of this mini epidemic, more than 1,000 civilians were infected.

Many prisons are ill equipped to recognize or treat TB. Inmates with chronic coughs are written off as smokers or other problems. Because TB spreads so quickly through shared air, many prison systems have implemented full-scale testing programs over the past few years, although enforcement of the testing programs is often lacking, so many potentially infected inmates slip through the cracks.

The same is true with inmates who refuse to be tested for HIV. They leave prison not knowing if the needles they have shared in prison or the sex they have had there left them tagged with a deadly disease.

Correction departments that run their own infirmaries and hospitals generally resist outside intervention or involvement. Even public health officials have difficulty gaining access to these facilities.

The overriding need to address the problem of overcrowding must be managed before many of the associated problems can be put into check.

Overcrowding casts a host of negative effects on inmates. It opens the doors to competition for limited resources, aggression, higher rates of illness and contagious diseases, increased likelihood of recidivism, and higher suicide rates. Redesigning prisons and developing alternatives to incarceration can help stem the out-of-control overcrowding of our state prisons.

Prisoners are affected by the amount of space allocated to them and by the number of people with which they must share that space.

Personal control over their environment and the quality of the space itself mitigates the negative impact of space.

In chronically crowded conditions, inmates already prone to anti-social behavior experience idleness and boredom and a loss of personal control within their assigned spaces. Research shows that overcrowding has three types of effects on the daily prison environment.

First, since there is less space and fewer resources to be shared, inmates must learn to stretch them further. There is less of everything to go around, so the same space and resources must be stretched even further.

Inmates often find that their opportunities to participate in self-improvement and rehabilitative programs, such as academic, employment, and vocational training are eliminated. Prison officials use the management problem tack to justify cutbacks, but often they are made because officers just don't want to be bothered.

Overcrowding also jeopardizes work opportunities, leading more and more inmates into a state of forced idleness, which breeds discontent that can lead to behavioral problems.

Double-cell occupancy in overcrowded prisons invites a number of problems found less often in single-cell facilities. Inmates, often mismatched, face frustration when inmates have access to resources (food, supplies, etc.) and others do not. Conflicts can arise and aggression or violence escalates if not resolved.

The second effect of overcrowding is on the individual inmate's behavior. Stress thresholds are crossed frequently; prisoners handle stress differently, through withdrawal, aggression or depression.

Double-celled inmates often lose their ability to maintain their personal identity or have difficulty adjusting to unwanted inmate interaction, noise, and other disruptions to his space. These problems compound stress in overcrowded situations.

The impact on social relations and interaction is one of the most important effects of prison overcrowding. Crowded environments foster more aggression and competition, less cooperation, less social interaction.

Some inmates in those situations withdraw socially, adopting a defensive or guarded attitude in the process.

The third effect of overcrowding comes from the correctional system's inability to solve the space and related problems. In trying to solve both problems, some facilities classify prisoners on the basis of space rather than security level. This violates the standardization of offender classification for security purposes, but the process is routinely practiced.

In addition to the problems found in space and resources, overcrowding slows an inmate's progress through the system.

Crowding affects every inmate that lives in that environment. Some learn to cope, but others, unable to cope, contribute to higher rates of psychiatric commitment, illness complaints, and increased recidivism. The rates for suicide and other violent deaths are more prevalent during overcrowded periods.

It is interesting to note that despite the negative effects of overcrowding, it does not affect all prisons equally. Larger facilities with younger inmates fare better in crowded conditions. Responses also vary with racial, ethnic, and socioeconomic groups.

Medical

Taxpayers pay billions of dollars to private prison healthcare firms, like CMS—the nation's largest, which provides healthcare to hundreds of thousands of inmates in Illinois and dozens of other states. Overcrowding, as we have stated, lays fertile ground for the spread of disease and violence, endangering inmates and the public alike.

Companies like CMS are on the front lines of prison healthcare, which eventually affects public health. The quality of care is highly suspect, however, because of the preoccupation with the bottom line, the profit margin, of the corporation (the same as the preoccupation in private prison building companies).

For a company paid a fixed rate, every dollar NOT spent on healthcare finds its way in the company's profit column. This pursuit of profits has led to dishonest practices in our prisons.

One doctor in a maximum-security prison urged the wife of an inmate there to get "60 Minutes" to investigate the healthcare at that prison. The x-ray machine was made in 1959, and other equipment and supplies were barely usable or inferior in quality.

Inmates have died because the medical staff ignored critical symptoms, such as chest pains and shortness of breath. One inmate went to the infirmary complaining of chest pains. The nurse told him to return to work. He came back a while later, still complaining of chest pains. The nurse gave him a Tylenol and told him to go back to work. The third time when he barely made it to the infirmary with the help of another inmate, he was told to lie on a gurney in the hallway. He died there an hour later, before anyone did anything.

Red tape often delays treatment in life-threatening situations when the staff is not up to capacity, when no physician is present, and when the skeleton crew must seek and secure permission to move an inmate out of the prison to an outside hospital.

"We save money because we skip the ambulance and bring them right to the morgue," said one nurse implicated in the wrongful death of a Florida inmate. It might be funny if it were not so close to the truth. Inmates routinely die due to neglect, understaffing, improperly trained or qualified staff, indifference, or overzealous cost cutting.

One inmate, who suffered a critical hernia problem, sued the medical staff for negligence. When one nurse on staff backed his claim, she was fired. Prisoners cannot choose their healthcare provider, doctor or treatment program. He also has no advocate to come to his rescue. It's a crapshoot. The healthcare providers have a captive audience made up of misfits that many in society regard as throwaways.

The substandard health care rendered by physicians in most prisons today offends the Hippocratic Oath, which they took to keep "free from all intent the wrongdoing and harm", no matter where they work. Someone needs to give these doctors a refresher course in that oath.

But who are these doctors anyway? One of the cost-saving measures practiced by private healthcare companies is the hiring of physicians who have failed in their private medical practices or even have committed crimes. One doctor on record stated that doctors in the latter category serve their prison time attending to inmates.

So, doctors who cannot practice medicine on the general public are hired for low wages to work in a situation where they are legally not allowed to prescribe the most common painkiller.

One big problem with private healthcare providers in the prison setting is that there is no watchdog, little accountability, and, as a result, too much substandard care and too many wrongful deaths.

The Wrongful Death Institute in Missouri monitors wrongful deaths and intervenes for surviving family members in legal hassles and lawsuits that often follow.

The prison population is land mine. With people serving longer sentences, they are going to develop the health problems that go with aging. The longer they remain in prison, the more likely they will develop serious healthcare problems that drastically increase the costs of supporting them.

In a surprising boost to prisoners' rights, on January 10, 2006, the United States Supreme Court ruled unanimously that prisoners could sue for damages over inhumane cell conditions and other cruel and unusual punishments. The decision [No. 546U.S.2006] came by way of the case involving a Georgia inmate who said he was confined to a cell so small he could not turn around his wheelchair or reach the toilet without help. He filed his lawsuit under the Americans with Disability Act; Title II of the Act bars any public entity from discriminating against any qualified individual with a disability.

In Illinois, by reducing 1,300 front-line corrections officers, remaining officers and prisoners are at risk of being maimed or killed. Legal costs to the state could easily exceed the cost of running the prison at Thomson, knowing that prisons are at 168 percent and understaffed. It is not negligent. It constitutes willing and wanton disregard for life.

The governor has stated recently that the incidence of violence in prisons has dropped 35 percent. The state is getting by with that because of the way it classifies an incident in the prisons. If one prisoner slaps another prisoner, it can be recorded as an assault or turn a blind eye.

So, the state can massage those statistics up or down. In my opinion, if the classification guidelines change, statistics reporting can be manipulated.

Waste Issues:

1.   *Overcrowding state prisons to the detriment of inmates and risk of prison staff and community citizens*

2.   *Providing substandard physical and mental healthcare and treatment to inmates*

3.   *Failing to consolidate smaller, less efficient prisons and transferring prisoners to more cost-effective prisons to alleviate the problem of overcrowding.*

4.   *Ignoring the real threat of lawsuits by inmates for inhumane cell conditions and cruel and unusual punishment. [A wrongful death lawsuit in Illinois could run from $100,000 to $500,000, another taxpayer burden.]*

8

THE THREE WASTES OF INCARCERATION: HUMAN, SOCIAL & MORAL

Building more prisons to address crime
is like building more graveyards to
address a fatal disease.

Robert Gangi
Executive Director
Correction Association of New York

We have reviewed the incalculable waste of taxpayer dollars in our criminal justice system, but dollars alone do not give the full picture of waste in the system. In this chapter, we delve deeper into the waste of human lives (and their potential), social waste (disruption of the family unit and abandonment of children), and moral waste (loss of freedom and lack of forgiveness).

The waste of human lives

Cost escalation in our prison system starts, of course, with the cost of human lives, lives lost in a system of injustice, unfair representation, corruption, and greed. The 164th person in the United States to be freed through post-conviction DNA testing was recently released from a prison in Georgia after spending 25 years behind bars. It never mattered that men like him declared their innocence all the years they served.

In a sampling of 110 men sentenced to death row and later found—through DNA evidence—that they were as innocent as they first claimed they were, two-thirds (62) were black or Hispanic. That figure accurately reflects the racial mix of the state prisons.

These men most likely came from impoverished or working class families and they were denied the prime of their lives, when they could have worked and earned good wages and supported their families. Collectively, they spent 1,149 years in prison. It is an egregious waste of human life and taxpayer dollars.

Lives not lost through execution or wrongful conviction are gradually eroded, due to the inhumane conditions of most prisons. Offenders fall prey to sexual predators and experience physical abuse and intimidation. The problems of overcrowding and double bunking, as mentioned earlier, add to the difficulties already characteristic of life in confinement.

The emergence of 'supermax' prisons designed to lock prisoners in single cells for prolonged periods of time has raised new issues. Years of isolation in a tiny 'seg' cell create new problems for inmates and officers alike. Some men break under the pressure and manifest mental illness. These prisoners, more than those in general population, are more likely to receive insufficient attention to their physical and mental health problems.

Consider that 700,000 or more men and women currently incarcerated in prisons throughout the United States will return to society. That's 700,000, plus. Some of them will be released from supermax prisons, where they have suffered mental breakdowns and nurtured anger and resentment. Our taxes have supported a system that warehouses men and women without looking at the big picture—their release back into society. It is a waste of human lives for these prisoners not to have received mental and physical health care, counseling, and extensive therapy. It is a waste of our tax dollars. It is a national outrage.

Prisons, which should concentrate on rehabilitation and preparation of prisoners to return to society, instead perpetuate crime. It's almost as though they encourage criminal tendencies; for the most part, officers look the other way when it comes to prisoner rape, theft, and other aggressive behavior. Their prime concerns are to prevent prisoners from escaping, protect against injury to themselves and others, and make black market money on drugs, tobacco and other contraband.

Again, we waste the taxpayers' money supporting a system that tolerates criminal behavior and does little to turn it around. It also wastes opportunities for prisoners to learn the value of rejecting crime and embracing a better, safer way of life.

Aging and critically ill inmates

In a recent Detroit News article, the problem of Michigan's aging prisoners was presented with some grim statistics for taxpayers. Forget about housing prisoners (where the annual average cost is $25,000). Their medical care is what is burning a hole in the taxpayers' pockets.

Money spent to pay for the high costs of medical care for prisoners could be better spent on schools and other social programs. In fact, the annual budget for housing an elderly inmate is $69,000, according to the National Center of Institutions and Alternatives. Most of these inmates, if released, would qualify for Medicare or Medicaid, which would transfer the financial burden from the states to the federal government.

The health problems of elderly inmates mirror those of adults in a free society: diabetes, epilepsy, cancer, amputations, HIV, Parkinson's, hepatitis C, Lou Gehrig's disease, and kidney and liver failure. Many prisoners undergo major operations, including heart transplants and open heart surgery.

Health care for Michigan prisoners jumped 50 percent in six years, from $120 million to $181 million. This crisis is avoidable, because the very people who are absorbing these astronomical tax dollars are the ones least likely to repeat crime should they be released.

According to U.S. Department of Justice Statistics from 1990, only 2 percent of men paroled after the age of 55 return to prison. That, in contrast to men ages 18-24, which shows a 22 percent recidivism rate.

Michigan taxpayers can thank former Governor John Engler [and his successor Jennifer Granholm] for this financial crunch. In the 1990s, Engler made the Michigan Parole Board one of the toughest in the nation, appointing members who were not big on rehabilitation. In 1992, inmates with life sentences had to serve 15 years to become eligible for parole, and then it was no guarantee. They also had to wait five years between bids for parole. In 1998, the state passed a law requiring inmates to serve their minimum sentences, if not more.

Department of Justice Statistics show that recidivism rates among elderly offenders is minimal, as low as 1-2 percent. Removing the elderly from prisons, relocating them in either minimum-security facilities or securing housing for them outside the walls could alleviate some of the problems of overcrowding. Clearly, they are not a threat to society.

The financial cost of incarcerating senior citizens nationwide challenges the imagination. All the trappings of aging, including eyeglasses, hearing aids, medications, and therapies, often for chronic or terminal diseases, magnify the basic cost of incarceration.

The psychological stress of incarceration accelerates aging in men and women who may have compromised their health before their arrest. More than non-inmates with the same illnesses, they tend to get sicker, partly because diagnosis and treatment are delayed by the intricacies of incarceration. Aging inmates are especially vulnerable to diabetes, heart disease, and hepatitis.

California spends two to three times more a year housing inmates over the age of 55. The number of senior prisoners is growing, as more men and women are incarcerated for longer terms. From the 1950s to 1971 California operated the nation's first prison for elderly inmates. Although old felons today are housed through the system, studies show that mingling them with the general prison population costs more than if they were housed in special units.

Time to let go

When a prisoner is tied to monitoring devices, dependent on oxygen or undergoing corrective surgeries, it is time to rethink policies that mandate that the prisoner serve his full term of incarceration. Although a prisoner, when he was younger, may have committed bank robberies or even murder, when he reaches the point where he is no longer a risk to society, save a burden on the taxpayer, it is time to open the gate and let him out. If nothing else, it makes room for a younger criminal on the street that should be locked up or, if not that, it releases tax dollars that could be used for education or social programs in the community.

Hard-liners disagree, of course, because they're part of the system that caused the problem and they're benefiting by the corruption.

In the meantime, the waste mounts up. Programs suffer, from highways to high schools, because taxpayers are carrying the heavy burden of supporting elderly, sick inmates.

If California, for instance, continued to admit 1,200 'three-strikes' felons annually, by 2026 there will be 30,000 of them serving 25 to life at a cost of $750 million a year. And the state pays the tab for their healthcare.

An old, blind and mentally ill death row inmate, executed there recently, appealed to the governor in his state for a stay, stating that executing such a person is cruel and unusual punishment based on the United States Constitution. The cost of housing the second oldest prisoner (he just passed his 76th birthday before being executed) for many years, his legal appeals for relief, and his healthcare far outweighed his threat to society. Execution removed one more from the prison rolls, but the gap was immediately filled with another.

The process involved in gaining the release of an elderly, sick prisoner is a jumble of red tape that discourages many from trying to unravel it. Approvals upon approvals must be secured, especially if the prisoner is a lifer. Some states have proposed to follow California's earlier example and set up minimum-security prisons or units within existing prisons to house geriatric prisoners. Staffing would be less expensive, as fewer officers and other staff personnel would be needed. For those who have families to go home to, another option would be to have them home-monitored. If it's good enough for a healthy Martha Stewart, it's good enough for a sick or aging prisoner.

The release of many elderly prisoners would shift the financial burden of their health and welfare from the state to the federal budgets, and free state funds not only to help balance the budget, but pay for schools, parks, and highways.

Many advocates of the elderly in prison believe that 'three-strikes' reform is the only long-term solution. States need to take a second look at their sentencing policies and examine what causes people to commit crimes in the first place. In fact, many states have already overturned their tough sentencing laws.

Mentally ill inmates

One of 10 inmates is mentally ill. In some states, 3 percent of the entire state prison population could be classified as certifiably mental.

In the 1970s and 1980s, large mental hospitals around the country were closed under the theory that patients would be provided "care in the community."

Unfortunately, financially strapped communities were not able to assume care of their mentally challenged residents, who drifted into a life of crime and ended up in prison. Prisons have since then have become "de facto mental hospitals," according to former correctional psychologist Thomas Fagan, Ph.D.

In many cases, prison worsens the condition of the mentally ill—especially in overcrowded settings—by the time they return to society.

Collectively, prisoners harbor a host of problems, from abuse to addiction, from illiteracy to mental illness. Prison provokes many of those problems, but for prisoners who demonstrate more than one of those problems, the outlook is indeed grim.

To add to the problem, 17 percent of our prisons do not conduct mental health tests on their inmates or offer any comprehensive therapy programs. Ten percent of Iowa's prisoners are mentally ill, yet the state DOC provides only three psychiatrists for more than 8,000 prisoners. Wyoming's system has only one on duty—two days each month. As a result of this lack of testing and treatment, mental illness goes unchecked in a general population.

Mentally ill inmates are controlled by psychotropic drugs and relegated to punishment blocks year after year, according to a study of the New York DOC Services. More than 25 percent of the inmates in New York are diagnosed with mental illness; half of them attempted suicide while imprisoned. In Indiana, approximately 3 percent of the state's 26,000 prisoners might be considered certifiable, but that 3 percent is costing taxpayers dearly. Psychotropic drugs used to control them are not cheap and those in the 3 percent range do not work, further adding to the taxpayer burden.

Twenty percent of all inmates are so obviously deranged that even prison medical personnel acknowledge their mental illness. In virtually all prisons, mentally ill prisoners are housed with the general population, where they are financially and sexually exploited by other convicts.

Some, if not all, of these mentally ill prisoners, need institutionalization, but that should not be in a prison setting.

All kinds of problems happen when the mentally ill go to prison. Corrections officials turn a blind eye and seriously medicate them. Those that are uncontrollable are housed in lockup facilities. Those who are mentally ill but controllable spend their days on idle or in drug lines waiting for their next dose of psychotropic drugs. The policy dictates that health workers check the prisoner's mouth to make sure he has swallowed the pill. Remember some medications induce a kind of euphoria, so prisoners often tuck the pills in their mouths where no one will notice and remove them later and sell them to the general population for the desired intoxication effect. That is a form of abuse.

Mentally ill prisoners housed with the general population pose other safety, health, and social problems. When they opt not to take their medications, they rant loudly, often out of a sound sleep, disturbing other inmates. They are known to urinate and defecate on the floor and not clean up after themselves. Aggressive behavior and occasional violence can erupt from these inmates when they receive hostile reactions to their disturbing habits.

Sadly, the states that have undergone aggressive prison building campaigns have sacrificed taxpayer dollars to do so that might have gone into mental health and treatment programs. Now, the mentally ill in prison are relegated to cells with little ability to become rehabilitated, educated or skilled in a trade. Every day is a challenge for these people.

It would be far better to consider housing the nation's 440,000 mentally ill prisoners in lower-security facilities that need not be so heavily staffed and would likely save taxpayer dollars. For whatever peace of mind is available to these prisoners, they would more likely find it in a place designed to give them less hostility and misery.

In the meantime, we have situations where mentally ill prisoners are housed on death row and even executed, despite considerable outcry against executing the mentally ill. In 1992, just before the New Hampshire primary, then-governor Bill Clinton returned to Arkansas deliberately to preside over the execution of Ricky Ray Rector, a mentally ill patient. He was clinically insane but legally qualified to be executed.

Thankfully, in 2005, Indiana Governor Mitch Daniels handled that issue differently. He commuted the death sentence of a mentally ill prisoner who has a treatable medical disorder. Hal Taylor, president of Citizens for Effective Justice wrote laudatory letter to Daniels, in which he made a strong case for the mentally ill. "Mentally ill people who are receiving treatment tend to be law abiding, non-violent, and respect the rights of others. Untreated mentally ill people can be delusional and can have impaired judgment that can lead to acts of violence against innocent people, even homicide. Killing a person with a treatable medical disorder who has killed someone else will do nothing to deter criminal acts by others."

Taylor calls for effective treatment as the "only evidence-based practice that can stop capital crimes by the mentally ill. Treatment needs to be made available to all who need it regardless of their ability to pay. If access to treatment is denied for whatever reason and the mentally ill person commits murder while in a disordered state, then responsibility lies more with the authorities who denied treatment than with the mentally impaired individual."

There is now an "enormous, unusual agreement among police, prison officials, judges, prosecutors, and human rights lawyers that something has gone painfully awry with the criminal justice system" notes the co-author of a 2003 Human Rights Watch report on mentally ill prisoners. The voice of the opposition to our current system of incarceration is growing, and it crosses political and socioeconomic lines.

Some rays of hope appear on the horizon, however. Legislators in some states are drafting bills to support the funding of mental health courts, similar drug courts already in existence. For a guilty plea, mentally challenged offenders would be sentenced to treatment instead of prison. That policy, already in operation in California, has lowered recidivism rates in drug courts by 77 to 85 percent. It is hopeful that a similar policy would reverse the tide of mass incarceration of the mentally ill.

Social waste

Society pays a high price for the excessive incarceration of its fellow citizens. The greatest victims might well be the children of the incarcerated. With almost two million children having a parent behind bars, the resultant damage is difficult to calculate.

Most of these children are from poor minority families living in marginal communities. When mandatory minimum sentencing swept the streets of low-level drug offenders, countless children became orphaned of at least one parent, sometimes both parents.

Taxpayers pay double in situations like these. First, they pay for the incarceration of the parent(s), and then they pay for the housing and care of juveniles left behind. Juvenile hall residency runs at about $5,000 a month, and living in a children's home can double that amount.

More than money is a stake when we imprison low-level criminals and dispatch their children to juvenile justice or state welfare agencies. These children are 'at risk' for all sorts of misbehavior, including truancy, teenage pregnancy, drug use, gang membership, and crime. They see the injustice of the system when a parent is given a sentence that does not fit the crime. Rebellion often follows.

The problem is complicated when the children of imprisoned parents enter a life of crime and follow in their footsteps. It is likely that legislators and policymakers, who prefer to build prisons and extend sentences to secure votes and satisfy the bottom line, would adequately address this problem.

Child psychologists understand that children of parents in prison suffer loss, no differently than those who lose a parent to death or abandonment. They experience depression, anger, and guilt and for the very young, a feeling feel that they have been abandoned. Many of them demonstrate PTSD (Post-Traumatic Stress Disorder) that produces depression, sleep difficulties, eating disorders, and nightmares.

Although young children often suffer in silence, older children of the incarcerated act out their moods and feelings through more aggressive behavior and anger that leads to disciplinary problems and delinquency.

Moral waste

For the 67 percent of parents in federal prison on non-violent drug charges with an average sentence of 10 years, their children's experience can be morally damaging. They may lose respect for the legal system that brought unwarranted prison sentences to their parents that caused traumatic familial separation and untold attendant problems.

Many consider a country like North Korea to be an oppressive nation, yet we lock up our poor, uneducated, addicted masses at rates that alarm the most oppressive countries of the world. We deny justice to many victims of the War on Drugs. Of the two million or more Americans in prison, 90 percent are high school dropouts and 92 percent are functionally illiterate. Those are appalling statistics and a moral disgrace for the world's wealthiest country.

What is the moral waste of denying basic human and civil rights to more than two million of our people, marginalized by life's circumstances and punished by a system that does not treat lawbreakers equally?

The moral waste of unnecessary and unjustly prolonged incarceration is evident in figures comparing the financing of prisons vs. schools. Most states spend, on average, $5,500 per year to educate a youth and as much as $30,000 a year to imprison a young person. Again, most of those who suffer the negative effects of this lopsided system are minorities, especially young African American males.

Where is our moral obligation to give citizens of a nation founded on freedom, liberty, and justice their basic human and civil rights? The answer to this question is imperative if we are to advance as a nation and fulfill to the promises of our founding fathers.

Americans are a forgiving people. When presidents, movie stars, and corporate chiefs fall from the pedestals on which we place them, we tend to forgive their indiscretions and failings. We are not quite so quick to forgive those who come from lower stations in life. It is time to reinstate forgiveness in our efforts to rehabilitate non-violent and drug/alcohol-addicted offenders. It is time to practice forgiveness and compassion for the poor, elderly, infirm, and for the children born into those unfortunate circumstances.

Waste Issues:

1.   *Incarcerating far too many non-violent and drug offenders for long sentences*

2.   *Prolonging the incarceration of elderly, infirm prisoners*

3.   *Substituting prisons for mental hospitals to warehouse mentally ill individuals*

4.   *Ignoring the emotional and psychological needs and problems of children of the incarcerated, who are likely to follow a life of crime*

9

REHABILITATION & RECIDIVISM
THE REVOLVING DOOR

There are some duties we owe even
to those who have wronged us.
There is, after all, a limit to
retribution and punishment.

Cicero
106BC – 43BC

For every liberal that believes rehabilitation of prisoners works, there are dozens of naysayers. In one respect, their negative opinions ring true. Statistics abound that show recidivism (return to prison within two or three years of release) is alive and well in our state prison systems. So what does the terms 'correctional' mean? Most prison systems utilize that tag as part of their official names.

While our prison system has come a long way from the Quaker method that insisted on absolute silence and total penitence, we have still not applied ourselves in delivering a system that 'corrects' or rehabilitates individuals destined, in large part, for return to society. Rehabilitation, which should be the number one priority in state (and federal) prisons, has given way to warehousing convicts, often stripping them of programs that exercise their bodies and expand their minds.

History has shown that when programs are discontinued, prisoners often take out their frustrations on fellow inmates, officers, and prison staff members. Violence increases and often leads to individual assaults or widespread rioting that leads to death. Riots in prisons like Attica and Indiana State Prison in the past have forced the system to instate or reinstate educational and recreational programs for prisoners.

Americans should ask themselves, would I want my new neighbor to be someone just released from prison? True, not all ex-convicts or even ex-felons make bad or threatening neighbors, but without adequate measures for rehabilitation in prison, they emerge from a dark hole with little incentive to become upstanding, productive members of society. We need to start making sure our tax dollars are spent on rehabilitation of those prisoners most likely to be released into our communities, for their sake and for ours.

"What I'm seeing is people coming out of prison with anywhere from moderate to severe symptoms of post-traumatic stress disorder (PTSD)," notes Bonnie Kerness, associate director of the American Friends Service Committee's Criminal Justice Program in New Jersey. "People are coming out with hair-trigger tempers."

It's becoming more and more difficult to survive the harsh conditions of prison life. Hard times have gotten much harder. Just ask any lifer. Rehabilitation and recreation, once generously offered, have given way to segregation and isolation. It's enough to drive any man mad. The harder their life is in prison, the more difficult it is for them to adjust on the outside.

Instead of making prisoners less likely to commit crimes after getting out, our system seems to foster the opposite. There is no deterrent effect; rather, there is an increased likelihood that ex-offenders will return to prison. "Incarceration can move the prisoner to a more serious level of criminal activity as a result of association with other more serious offenders," notes noted criminologist Alfred Blumenstein. It's like prison is a graduate school of crime, and there are too many prisoners getting degrees.

Rehabilitation

Some states, like California, essentially banned rehabilitation from their corrections systems, only to eventually see the error of their ways—an increase in crime, increase in prison population, and a higher recidivism rate.

Most corrections officers prefer education and recreation programs for inmates. These activities—pursing a GED or college degree or achieving first place in a prison weight-lifting competition—constructively occupy time for prisoners. They channel their energies in mental or physical pursuits that have some redeeming value. They acquire some self-esteem in the process, too. They become more passive and less likely to act aggressively or violently toward other inmates or officers.

Regardless of legislative or corrections policy about rehabilitation, many state constitutions recognize that the foundation of their penal systems is reformation, not vindictive justice. To deny rehabilitation as a means of reforming prisoners is to deny them their constitutional rights. As Robert Gangi so aptly says, "People go to prison as punishment, not for punishment." Not providing rehabilitation opportunities in the prison system is another form of punishment.

Twenty or more years ago many state corrections systems pursued rehabilitation of their prisoners. One such state—Indiana—clearly demonstrated that a professionally managed program within prison walls could dramatically rehabilitate prisoners and reduce recidivism at the same time.

Dr. Charles Musgrave served as director of the music department at Indiana State Prison for 22 years, retiring in the mid-1990s. In the 22 years of his music program, more than a thousand men participated. A more amazing fact is that only three (3) prisoners of the 1,000-plus who participated ever returned to prison after being released.

Dr. Musgrave credits that stunning success rate to the fact that he instilled values in his program participants that were applicable on the outside. "I did not encourage them to pursue careers in music after they left prison. Rather, I challenged them to utilize the skills music gave them to make them good, productive citizens in whatever careers they chose."

Five of the skills these inmates learned in the music program bear mentioning:

1. They learned delayed gratification, something quite foreign to men who were accustomed to receiving instant gratification when they were on the streets. In music, they had to work to achieve a goal.

2. They learned tolerance. Music transcends racial lines and embraces people of all colors and creeds. According to Dr. Musgrave, one of the early bands in his department combined talented musicians of different colors and from a variety of cultures and backgrounds. "It was about music or the making of a musician, not about racial pride or prejudice."

3. They learned parenting/mentoring by helping each other learn or develop a musical skill. This skill was something they could pass on to their children when they got out.

4. They learned responsibility. They had to carry their share of the load and be ready or they set the rest of the band back.

5. They learned leadership. "Whenever I saw leadership potential, I fostered it," says Musgrave. Inmate leadership can rise to the top, as in Texas, where inmates run the music department, largely because the state won't pay an outsider to do so.

What impact can a music program have on inmates who participate in it? When Dr. Musgrave became music director, he knew what to do. "I made a deal with the warden. I would give a concert every two weeks all summer from May 1 to the end of October, the 'hot season' when most riots take place in prisons. He agreed. One week it would be Cell House A, and two weeks later, Cell House B. Everyone in Cell House B would be after those in A to not mess up or they wouldn't get their chance.

"From that, we held open houses in the prison auditorium, and the families of inmates attended. The men got to see their wives on a different basis than in the visiting room. That's when they really tried to be on their best behavior, because they didn't want to lose that opportunity.

"For 14 years, there were no lockdowns. It was history in the making, as that prison had the only classically run music department in the entire country. Well, our music department finally got too well known. We'd be on Indiana and Chicago radio stations. One day, after a radio station in Indianapolis aired one of our programs, Gordon Faulkner, the DOC commissioner at the time, came to me and said, 'If I ever read another story about your music department or hear these guys on the radio, you'll never work another day here. We're here to house these men, not to entertain them or educate them.' He was a transplant, who brought the Texas Mafia to strong-arm corrections in Indiana."

The music department had an outstanding success rate of placing men on the street and keeping them there. That has been one of the unheralded characteristics of the music program.

Inmates who are sincere about music can endure the demands placed on them by many hours of practice, which make good performances possible. The traits demanded in music are readily transferable to success "on the street".

Some of the demands of people successful in society are responsibility, punctuality, and working hard, setting set short-term and long-term goals, and concentrating on achieving those goals. Add to those traits honesty, an even-tempered personality, and the ability to delay gratification, and a prisoner can achieve his goals in prison and apply the same traits after he gets out of prison.

Success stories similar to Dr. Musgrave's can be told countless times in prisons across the country. Myopic mentalities close programs when instead they deserve to remain open and replicated throughout our system.

One success story

After serving almost 20 years in Indiana prisons, Chris Milford, now 48 years old, clearly remembers his years in Dr. Musgrave's music department. Chris played sax and drums in different bands, participated in musical programs, and served as Musgrave's right-hand man, repairing equipment and handling other responsibilities in the department.

"When Charlie first came aboard, the music department was in a dilapidated building that should have been condemned. The administration did not look on the music department favorably, but more as a babysitter, a distraction to keep convicts occupied.

"Eventually, the department moved to the renovated education building and acquired considerable space, carpeted floors, soundproof walls, and several practice rooms for individuals and groups.

"Charlie had one requirement. Everyone had to take a music theory class and pass it in order to stay in the department. Of course, you also had to have a clean record and good attitude.

"When I first went to prison, all I knew was anger. From parental sexual abuse as a child to a history of drugs and alcohol, I suffered low self-esteem. Charlie instilled dignity in his students and a feeling of self-worth. He would lecture us, 'You are not crap. You are worth something. If you set your mind to it, you can accomplish it.'

"He would always come up with 'Do you know how to get to Carnegie Hall?' We thought he was asking for directions. Instead, Charlie's response was, 'Practice.'"

And practice they did. They had swing and jazz bands, country bands, and soul music groups. "While we were in the music department, it was like we weren't in prison. We were free to express ourselves through music. Charlie also shared his Christian faith with us, teaching us respect and forgiveness. If we didn't feel like forgiving someone, he would take us to task about it."

In addition to being active in the music department, Dr. Musgrave encouraged his students to participate in group therapy, enroll in anger management courses, and pursue education.

Swiss Institute of Criminology

Founded in Geneva, Switzerland in 1975, the Swiss Institute of Criminology moved to the United States two years later. Dr. Stanley Showalter, a counseling psychologist and criminologist and one of the co-founders of the Institute, established an extended group therapy program at Indiana State Prison in 1978, under contract to the State of Indiana. Over the next 21 years, he would oversee group therapy for four groups per week, 8 or 9 men per group. The program was full most of those years, often with a two-page waiting list.

From the beginning, some prison administrators were overwhelmed with the scope of the program and were outspoken against treatment, including psychological counseling. Dr. Showalter did not publicize the program, knowing that publicity would be the death knell of the program. "That's counter logical."

The goals of the program were twofold: (1) help prisoners learn better tools to survive in prison. Some participants were double-lifers, who would never be released, so rehabilitation was not an issue for them; and (2) give prisoners the tools they would need to not return to prison after they were released.

The program was not a social group. Participants were expected to work toward their goals as long as they needed to.

"Self-esteem was one of the tools, and choice-making a strong second, like having the strength to avoid the people and environment they came from. Of course, anger management, which is now old hat, was one of the tools. We taught them to recognize the trigger that identified what made them angry and the message in their heads that gave them the wrong reaction. What, in that 8-second gap between trigger and reaction, could they do to alter their old responses?"

From 1983 to 1993, Dr. Showalter tracked the Institute's participants after they were released from prison. The success rate was truly remarkable—86 percent!

Despite this obvious ability to lower the rate of recidivism, Dr. Showalter and the program took constant heat from corrections officials and legislators; some wanted to investigate Dr. Showalter. "We could not have survived without the intervention of Ed Cohn, DOC Commissioner, who repeatedly stood up for the program. George Phend, a warden at Indiana State Prison, was instrumental in helping me open the psychology department in the first place, because he believed in the value of treatment."

The right stuff

At the age of 21, Edward, serving a life sentence, made an early determination that saved his life and gave him a new lease on life. To quote a common solution, he took lemons and made lemonade.

"I realized that my attitude toward confinement—right or wrong—determined how I was going to shape my life in the years ahead. I taught myself diction by looking into a mirror while I pronounced vocabulary words. I learned to articulate my thoughts clearly as a result."

Over the years, Edward enrolled in every trade and educational program offered by the prison back when the corrections system believed in rehabilitation. He learned CPR/First Aid and fire fighting, receiving certificates in both and saving several lives and buildings during his participation in those activities. He went on to become an accredited cook and baker, amassing thousands of hours of training and eventually becoming the head cook for the last prison in which he served before his release after almost 30 years. He also earned his Associates Degree from a major university.

The foundation of rehabilitation lies in one's heart and mind. It does not come from the institution or the prison staff. It starts with a desire to change, even if—as in Edward's case—he received an unjust sentence.

The majority of prisoners will eventually be released. It is important to remember that one might end up living near you. Do you want that ex-convict coming out angry and bitter to the point of taking it out on you or your children? Or do you think your tax dollars would be better spent doing everything possible to change his attitude and give him the tools needed to survive in a free society?

Tremendous waste exists in the so-called rehabilitation of inmates. By and large, programs designed to put anger in check or teach skills simply become another avenue to funnel money into the prison system. In one prison in the Midwest, by merely enrolling in an anger management course, the prison received thousands of dollars per prisoner, but the course did little to put anger in check. In fact, the course was so superficial, that many did not attend after enrollment brought in the mandatory bucks. So, the taxpayer dollars went for naught, save to line the pockets of the correctional system.

The same runs true with other programs, including re-integration courses that prisoners are required to take before they are released from some prisons. Again, the prison receives several thousand dollars per prisoner for enrolling in the course, even if the teachings are so common sense that most prisoners, regardless of the length of his sentence or intellect, would have to take the course to make it on the outside. Unless more substance is introduced into the program, meaningful insights and values passed on to inmates about to be released, our tax dollars again are wasted.

So if prisons do little, if anything, to rehabilitate prisoners and most inmates are not inclined to do as Edward did to turn their lives around, what can be done to stem the tide of recidivism? What is the key to removing the revolving doors from our prisons? More programs like Dr. Musgrave's and Dr. Showalter's would help, but most prisons these days are cutting back on educational and other rehabilitation programs.

It's a terrible waste to incarcerate men and women for determinate sentences, knowing they will one day be released into society and not give them valuable opportunities to become productive citizens. One of the problems is that many repeat offenders are illiterate, uneducated, drug-addicted, and often suffering from one mental illness or another. They have little self-motivation to turn their lives around, and prisons lack the proper staff to tackle such difficult life problems.

Education

We set contradictory goals. On one hand, we want men and women to leave prison better than when they went in, but we block efforts to improve their lives. Education is a perfect example.

According to the Bureau of Justice Statistics:

- 68 percent of state prison inmates did not receive a high school diploma

- Approximately 26 percent of state prison inmates completed their GEDs while incarcerated.

Education was once considered a primary tool to meaningfully occupy prisoners and reduce recidivism. An educated man—or woman—is less likely to return to criminal activities after release. Pell grants provided the means to help prisoners pursue a higher education.

In a move that underscores the contradictory nature of our approach to rehabilitation, the United States Congress recently voted to stop all Pell grants for prisoners, in one fell swoop ending their ability to achieve a higher education. It just doesn't make good sense.

First, we instill in prisoners that education is their ticket out of crime, perhaps their last straw of hope, and then we pull the rug out from under them. Hope keeps people alive. Educational programs for prisoners work, but some people argue they don't work to mask their own resentment about prisoners having access to better education subsidized by the government.

There should be no place in society for resentment or prejudice, particularly in the pursuit of education by any group of people, including prisoners. To ensure that our tax dollars are spent most wisely, we need to encourage education in our prisons. An education is the most valuable tool inmates will receive to assure productive and meaningful life on the outside.

The best thing we can do to cut costs of incarcerating men and women is to turn our attention to giving good education to young children, beginning in kindergarten. By becoming educated, their prospects for a crime-free life are enormous. That is true even with prisoners who earn advanced degrees while they are incarcerated. The recidivism rate for them is zero.

Prison jobs

Our prison system may not reflect the true definition of gulag when it comes to *forced* slave labor, but our prisons utilize slave labor often for their own nefarious ends.

True, prison jobs teach inmates valuable skills that can be used after they return to society, but those who have no skills and need them the most are shut out of prison industry jobs. It's all about education. Prison industries want inmates who have a high school education or GED equivalency, because it is difficult to teach them skills if they have no education. That is intimidating to a lot of prisoners, because they lack the rudimentary skills to participate.

Inmates, who work in prison industries, must pass English and math tests, and have to prove they can comprehend basic instructions. That eliminates many prisoners. Those who are shut out of industries try to find regular prison jobs that may start at 11 cents/hour. That's not *money*.

Indiana statute provides that prisoners working for minimum wage (in prison industries) have deductions taken for room and board and for child support. The balance goes into a trust account administered by the Department of Corrections until the prisoner is released. The kicker is that prisoners who work for private companies are not allowed to have personal bank accounts. The DOC, instead, reaps any APR that accumulates in the trust account held for all prisoners. They take 55 percent of the pay—45 for room and board and the rest for child support, even if the prisoner working in the prison factory has no children. That's how the state makes money.

"When you talk about prisoners having money, the officials in the Indiana DOC from the top down recognize that money brings powers," notes a former lifer. "In the 1970s, the lifers organization had 560 lifer members. Back then, we were able to make products (crafts and such) and sell them to the public. We held bake sales, too, and did whatever else we could do to raise money. We accumulated enough cash to retain the services of a lobbyist. We needed a lobbyist to take bills before the state House and Senate that would prompt them into creating legislation that would bring lifers under the current sentencing statute. That freaked the DOC out completely. The warden went ballistic. He seized our account, took all our money, so we had no voice. Our bills died and were never again re-introduced.

"Prison officials do not want prisoners to have money. When you talk about prison reform, you have to start with the political base, the top of the system. We tested those waters."

Prison industries

For those who are fortunate enough to have an education and job in prison industries, work there teaches them accountability, pride in performance, a healthy work ethic, cooperation and teamwork, and the ability to work under supervision.

Many, if not most, states utilize prisoners for the production of license plates, furniture, clothing, and other goods, including airline reservations. Due to pressure by unions, however, some states have curtailed jobs for private companies in their prisons.

The principle argument in favor of prison labor is that it teaches them skills that will help them re-enter society more successfully and become contributing members of the communities. The opposition expresses concern that cheap prison labor removes jobs from the market that unemployed people on the outside could perform.

The debate shows little sign of ending. In the meantime, states like Ohio remain committed to educating and training offenders. State officials see that policy as a way to reduce prison costs, minimize victimization, reduce crime and drug addiction, reduce recidivism, and enhance the life of their communities.

The Illinois prison industries, which manufactures everything from bed linens to picnic tables, is not supported by tax dollars. The program derives sufficient revenues from the sale of its products and services to make it self-supporting.

Ohio must be doing something right. Studies there indicate that inmates who leave the state's correctional facilities with job skills are 18 percent less likely to return to prisons than are inmates who did not. "They have learned many of the skills it takes to succeed, creating a smoother transition back into society," says Reginald A. Wilkinson, Ed. D, director of the Ohio Department of Rehabilitation and Correction. "It furthermore allows released inmates to support families that might currently depend on public assistance."

Inmate labor has had a positive effect on Ohio communities. The Ohio DOC is implementing one U. S. Department of Justice initiative that encourages partnerships between correctional systems and private-sector entities to manufacture products. "This is an excellent opportunity to develop public-private partnerships," Wilkinson explains. "Thus, the work stays in Ohio instead of being outsourced offshore."

Michigan's Prison Build Program educates and provides hands-on training to inmates in the building trades and horticultural industries. The program is a cooperative effort between state and local government, nonprofit organizations, and projects like Habitat for Humanity that uses prison labor to provide housing for low-income families.

More than constructing walls, cabinets and other housing components, building entire homes or designing landscape plans, inmates carve out careers. The Prison Build Program provides links to employers to help inmates find jobs and aftercare programs to assist them in their reintegration after release.

Inspired by Oregon's successful Prison Blues program, a Michigan legislator plans to push a bill to create a similar prison clothing industry there. He urged the Michigan DOC to conduct a study to show how it would work. The study revealed little if any threat to outside industries or workers. Most of the wash-and-wear pants sold in the United States are made or assembled in Costa Rica, China or other countries. The program would provide new jobs, primarily in sewing, but would also tap some of the creative people who want careers in the fashion industry.

The Prison Blues factory in Oregon has employed up to 100 inmates since 1989. They make jeans, sweatshirts, jackets, shirts, and apparel. It has become a self-sustaining, $18-million-a-year enterprise that sells to retail outlets in the United States and ships to Japan and Europe. The program also sells products through their Internet Web site, www. prisonblues.com.

Instead of putting anyone out of work in the community, Prison Blues boosts local businesses that supply raw materials and equipment. Work programs have reduced recidivism in Oregon by 24 percent.

Another advantage of the program is that inmates with skills and something constructive to do while in prison are less likely to cause trouble in prison and more likely to stay out. That's something to think about when you consider that more than 95 percent of people incarcerated eventually return to their communities.

Rehabilitation on the outside

Many rehabilitation programs exist on the outside to help the newly released prisoner get on with his life in a meaningful way and to not get caught in the revolving doors of prison.

SSD, Inc. in Kokomo, Indiana, has an impressive track record for keeping ex-convicts out of prison and juvenile offenders out of jail. Founded by Douglas McAdam in 2000, the program has processed 1,200 inmates with a return of only 75.

The program concentrates on education, although it does not stop with academics. Instead, the program deals with changing a prisoner's perceptions, which, in turn, changes feelings, actions, and reactions. Prisoners learn who they are, to what purpose they exist, how to live their lives, and how to get along with others.

Citizens for Effective Justice, based in Bloomington, Indiana, advocates for effective implementation of therapeutic justice, starting in its home territory of Monroe County. One of the founders, Rev. Hal Taylor, and others involved in the program strive to shift public and official attitudes and institutional practice away from punishment to restorative and therapeutic justice. They advocate against incarcerating the mentally ill and drug-addicts individuals, and show special concern for the children of inmates, that they not follow the same path as their parents.

The Center for Therapeutic Justice in Virginia strives to offset the negative effects of incarceration and how they often follow inmates out the gate. "A person's incarceration as punishment usually has no direct relationship to their crime and they leave prison uneducated, uninformed about alternative pro-social behavior or solutions, ashamed and stigmatized by the community, unprepared to re-enter family and community, and with no opportunity to express remorse, heal, and mature."

Major budget cuts have eliminated or reduced significant services in prisons, but the hype continues nonetheless. Services offered through parole and probation and in jails and prisons are less than 2percent of what is assessed, requested, and needed.

Upon release-transition-re-entry, an offender returns to a society that could not be more rejecting, more discriminating, more marginalizing or more of a permanent barrier for re-acclimation.

One ex-convict's thoughts

The following thoughts are from a former prisoner in the California system. He went through the Insight Prison Project, which works with San Quentin State Prison to learn to anchor insights into lasting behavioral changes. He wrote the men he left behind after he was released.

"No matter how many programs [a prisoner] may be involved in, when it's all said and done, the true test is when you're by yourself and the decision you make when nobody is around. You see we are all responsible for our destiny. Personal responsibility within is what really determines our future. The choices we make and the decisions we choose while on the outside are what matter the most.

"Programs are great and insightful and help us get focused while inside, but sooner or later each one of you will be free. You either come out better or worse. The choice is totally up to you! They may have your bodies now, but they don't have your minds. I was a hardcore drug addict for over 20 years and I no longer have any desire to use. Why? Because being free and making my own decisions is as good as it gets. Life and freedom are things I cherish now."

Recidivism

Recidivism rates are exceedingly high, currently topping out nationally at about 67 percent (for women, it is only 58 percent). According to the Bureau of Justice statistics, more than two-thirds of released prisoners are re-arrested within three years. These staggering recidivism figures reflect the failure of our criminal justice system to rehabilitate and reform. Although statistics show we have reduced crime, we have not prevented ex-offenders from re-offending.

Our criminal justice system is paying for its crime of participating in the political/media scam of building more prisons, locking up prisoners and throwing away the keys, and using the enormous expense of doing so to eliminate education and other rehabilitative programs. According to an Urban Institute study, by the middle of the 1990s, only 6 percent of the $22 billion spent on prisons went to prison programs, like vocational, educational, or life skills training.

Prisoners who participate in educational, vocational, and work programs have lower recidivism rates by as much as 20-60 percent over prisoners who do nothing to change their lives. The odds are greatly in favor of those prisoners becoming productive members of society, and that is good news for communities in which they are released or choose to live upon release.

Most ex-offenders find it difficult, if not impossible, to find meaningful work; that is, if they overcome the stigma that a felony conviction carries. Although parole offers little to help parolees reintegrate and remain free, ex-offenders released on parole stand a better chance of remaining free than those do who leave at the end of their determinate or mandated sentences.

We have paid dearly for the mess we're in, not just through our tax dollars, but through our complacency toward the millions of men and women who pass through our criminal justice system and come out no better than when they went it.

Waste Issues:

1. *Canceling rehabilitation programs that prove effective in changing lives and cut recidivism rates.*

2. *Taking away Pell grants for education, denying prisoners the ability to pursue an education in prison.*

3. *Misusing funds by perpetuating the revolving door. Every time a prisoner returns to prison, it costs the taxpayers $27,000 or more a year to keep him there. The key to cutting waste is to "correct" inmates so they leave prison prepared to support their families and themselves or the taxpayers will pay dearly again and again and again.*

10

GENTLE JUSTICE

We don't believe in an eye
for an eye. We are a bit more
civilized than that, I hope.

Kaisa Tammi-Moilanen
Governor, Open Ward
Finnish Prison

Imagine a prison where there are no walls or razor wire circling the perimeter of the facility, a prison where cameras and other electronic alert devices monitor movement instead. Imagine a prison with no iron gates, bleak cells, and forbidding passageways but instead living spaces like dormitories.

Imagine a prison with unarmed officers, wearing civilian clothes and no emblems or insignia that denote authority. Imagine a prison where the only guns available are locked in the warden's safe.

Imagine a prison where inmates and officers address each other by their first names, and where they counsel one another when problems arise. Imagine a prison where inmates often go home for visits near the end of their sentence, and where, in the interim, they enjoy the privacy of housing on the prison grounds where they can invite their families to visit for up to four days.

Living with the antithesis of this imaginary prison makes it difficult to realize that it is not imaginary after all. Prisons like this one are the rule in Finland. "We believe that the loss of freedom is the major punishment, so we try to make it as nice inside as possible," says a prison supervisor.

In little over 30 years, Finland turned its rigid, harsh prison system with one of Europe's highest rates of imprisonment into a system of gentle justice. Tapio Lappi-Seppala, director of Finland's National Research Institute of Legal Policy, explains how that dramatic change could happen.

"Finnish criminal policy is exceptionally expert-oriented. We believe in the moral-creating and value-shaping effect of punishment instead of punishment as retribution." More than 40,000 Finns have been spared prison over the past 20 years at savings of $20 million. The crime rate took a nosedive to one of the lowest levels in Scandinavia.

One prison director noted the three levels of control: the first is self-control (where the individual learns to control his anger or his use of drugs and/or alcohol so that he does not endanger others). The second is social control (where the individual who cannot control himself is put into an anger management or alcohol or drug treatment program to prevent him from graduating to a street criminal). The third level is officer control (where the individual, who has no self-control and has committed a crime against society must be locked up and placed under officer supervision).

"In Finland, we try to intervene at the first level so people won't get to the other two." Officers agree that the system works well for all concerned. In earlier harsher prison environment there, more prisoners tried to escape, there was more violence, and the prisoners were harder to control.

Solitary confinement up to 20 days goes to inmates as punishment for fighting or drug possession, but the normal term is from three to five days. Even that is avoided at all costs, by talking to the inmate and working out a resolution.

The big difference in the Finnish criminal justice system is that the courts hand down four different levels of the punishment: (1) fines, (2) probation, (3) community service, and (4) unconditional prison sentence. Prisoners usually are released after serving only half their terms. There is no death penalty in Finland.

In a country with over five million people, less than 3,000 are incarcerated at any one time or 52 for every 100,000 citizens. By comparison, the ratio is 724 per 100,000 in the United States and climbing.

The Sentences Enforcement Act of Finland sets requirements for prison service, as follows:

- *Punishment is a mere loss of liberty.* Other restrictions can be used as required for the security of the prisoner and prison.

- *Prevention of harm, promoting of placement into society.* Punishment shall be enforced so that it promotes a prisoner's placement in society.

- *Normality.* The penal institution must be so organized that it closely resembles those in the rest of society.

- *Justness, respect for human dignity, prohibition of discrimination.* Prisoners must be treated justly and respecting their human dignity.

- *Special needs of juvenile prisoners.* When implementing a sanction sentenced to a juvenile offender, special attention must be paid to the needs cause by the young offender's age and stage of development.

- *Hearing of prisoner.* A prisoner must be heard when a decision is made concerning his/her placement in dwelling, work or other activity.

Much of the credit for this remarkable system goes to politicians and the media for keeping their debates over criminal justice civilized. "Our newspapers are not full of sex and crime, and there is no pressure on me to get tough on criminals from populist-issue politicians like there would be in a lot of other countries," noted one legislator.

Another reason why Finns tolerate the gentle justice policy is that the government compensates crime victims, who would not feel that justice is better served by doling out severe punishment. "We don't believe in an eye for an eye," said one prison ward chief.

Finns pay a much higher rate of taxes than Americans do, yet they get much more valuable mileage for their tax dollars. Education, welfare, and healthcare is all state funded. Finns pay nothing for education at any level, including post-graduate studies in law and medicine.

Providing an environment for prisoners to maintain strong ties with their families, learn a skill transferable to the outside, and take advantage of any number of rehabilitation programs results in a low recidivism rate (30-50%). That is largely because of the Finnish belief that excessive punishment translates only into a body count by the end of the day. Criminal justice officials believe that 12 years is the maximum sentence needed to rehabilitate the majority of offenders, and most of them are released at the halfway point in their terms.

The Finnish criminal justice stands as one of the best and most successful in the world. Could it happen in America? With the situation as it now stands, only in our imaginations!

If we cannot reform the total system, maybe we can implement some worthwhile changes. In our next chapter, we examine alternatives to prison for punishment.

Waste issues:

1)   *missing the opportunity to restructure sentencing to allow non-violent offenders alternatives to prison*

2)   *wasting lives by handing down sentences far longer than needed for reformation*

3)   *causing the disintegration of the families of prisoners by not granting them generous opportunities to spend time together to keep the family ties strong*

11

Alternative Sentencing Options

*It isn't that there aren't alternative ways
presently available for dealing with those
who threaten us or break our laws.
However, at times, they seem largely futile,
if not actually counter-productive.*

Jerome G. Miller
President & Co-founder
The National Center on Institutions & Alternatives

Alternatives sentencing options come in a wide variety. Some merely detain prisoners for a prescribed period of time, while others force violent criminals to do hard labor in order to survive. Let us look first at some of these less desirable sentencing options.

Penal colonies/Labor camps

In many cultures, for instance, the penal colony or settlement is use to detain and punish violent criminals. In cultures where there is no rehabilitation for their prisoners, the settlements are known as gulags or internment camps. Most of the prisoners relegated to this type of punishment are lifers, and many are forced to work for their survival.

North America became one large penal colony under control of the British through a system of indentured servants. That lasted until the end of the American Revolution, but the British just switched continents, taking advantage of remote areas of Australia to satisfy their desire for penal colonies.

Forced slave labor camps, which gained a horrific reputation in the Soviet Union, remain the preferred punishment by some cultures for violent criminals. Siberia, known for its remoteness and harsh climate, served as the *gulag* under czars. Slave labor developed forestry, logging, and mining industries, construction trades, highways, and roads across Siberia.

Exile

Designating a state, part of a country, or a remote island for exiling violent criminals has worked for this country (Alcatraz) and other cultures. The suggestion has been made to develop some of the vast open spaces in the western part of the United States for incarcerating violent criminal lifers, setting them apart from non-violent offenders serving shorter sentences.

Nothing definitive has been done with this idea and it is unlikely anything will happen in the foreseeable future. Although the isolation of exile might be in order for the most violent criminals, others caught unjustly in that plan would suffer through further disintegration of their families.

Corporal punishment

Various forms of corporal punishment, from hanging to firing squads, have been used in America but abandoned for more humane methods of execution.

Other cultures, like those in the Islamic world, still practice public stoning and decapitation as a means of execution and deterrent to those who might consider embarking on a criminal life. There is no hard evidence to demonstrate that either method works effectively to deter crime.

In some specific cases of stoning, for instance, there has been such loud public outcry against it, that the practice in those cases was abandoned. Stoning and decapitation, the most extreme examples of corporal punishment, are unlikely to gain favor in more civilized parts of the world where the drive toward more humane treatment of prisoners is gaining ground.

Boot camps

For the juvenile offender not responding to discipline at home or school, boot camps offer a physically demanding, military-style regimen created to instill discipline and better values. Because sentences in boot camps are shorter than prison sentences, the costs of running boot camps are less over the long haul, although dollar for dollar they appear to cost the same.

The drawback to boot camps is their reputation for high recidivism rates, up to 75 percent, among juvenile graduates of boot camps. These harsh methods used to reform juveniles backfire and undermine the other good qualities of this program.

Home confinement

Martha Stewart made home confinement a household term and almost fashionable after she was released from a women's prison in West Virginia over a year ago. More and more criminal justice systems are seriously looking at home confinement as one alternative to imprisoning non-violent offenders, particularly young men and women, who pose no serious threat to society.

This alternative, and others that we will discuss in this chapter, make sense in view of the fact that it is impractical—financially—to incarcerate all criminals. Some other method of addressing the issues of overcrowded prisons and the misuse of community-based alternatives must be put into play.

The bottom line speaks for itself. Even if communities or states were to increase their numbers of parole and probation officers to handle home confinement or other forms of punishment, the cost of putting offenders through those programs is far less than incarcerating them in state prisons. On average, the cost of supervision someone on parole or probation is $2 to $3/day, whereas the per diem cost of incarceration is $45 or higher.

Community-based programs

Numerous community-based programs, from work programs to drug courts, all designed to keep people out of prison and work out their problems under the guidance of constructive alternatives.

Milwaukee instituted a program that allows non-violent young men destined for prison for drug offenses to participate a highly structured regimen that focuses on education, drug treatment, and counseling. After successful participation in the program, the young men are allowed to get jobs in the community, while spending their nights in a locked facility. It beats hard-core prison.

The incentive behind this program and others is to keep low-level, non-violent offenders out of prison. This saves lives and taxpayer dollars, making it a win-win situation. "All criminal offenses certainly deserve a response," notes David C. Anderson in his book *Sensible Justice: Alternatives to Prison.* "But why should it invariably be the penitentiaries that inflict so relentless a burden on taxpayers, turn lightweight offenders into more dangerous criminals, and do nothing to help them confront their basic problems?"

Alternative measures are far cheaper than incarceration—$2,500 for drug and alcohol treatment, and $6,000 for intensive supervision, according to the National Community on Community Corrections. To realize these savings, however, community programs must be vigilant in making sure people enter the programs that truly belong in them, not those who were never candidates for prison in the first place. An alternative is what it says—an alternative to prison.

Drug courts

The practice of drug courts, designed to determine if low-level drug cases should be charged criminally or diverted into approved drug treatment programs, started in Florida in the 1980s and spread quickly to other states. Today, there are tens of thousands of people receiving treatment instead of incarceration because of this innovative alternative program.

In 2001, California enacted a voter-approved initiative mandating treatment for first-time drug offenders instead of prison, a program that diverted as many as 36,000 people from prison to community-based treatment.

A 1999 study conducted by the Rand Corporation determined that drug treatment programs save about $10,000 per participant, which is three times higher than their costs. That appeals to taxpayers. Arizona represents classic proof. In 1998, the state's drug courts saved taxpayers $2.5 million by keeping 551 prisoners out of prison.

"Drug courts are being smart on crime," notes a former Michigan police officer turned district attorney. "We are approaching 50 babies who were born crack-free and without fetal alcohol syndrome because their mothers were in the program." Michigan saves up to $500,000/child in health-care and social services costs.

Other Alternatives

Early parole

When a state's prison system reaches an alarming state of overcrowding, operating at any level above 100 percent, parole boards should consider reducing the sentences of low-level, non-violent offenders, granting them early parole. Early release would eliminate the problems of overcrowding and save money.

Sentencing discretion

Although some states are leading the way toward returning sentencing discretion to judges, more need to follow. Judges should also have the authority to hand down concurrent sentences instead of consecutive sentences.

Violent criminals belong behind bars, but not people who steal pizza. We need to bring sentencing guidelines into conformity with crime categories. Reducing the number of people sent to prison and reducing the number of years they have to serve is an excellent way to save money. California figured savings in the neighborhood of $750 million in incarceration costs simply by fixing its 'three strikes' law.

Revocation of 'truth in sentencing'

Under this law, prisoners had to serve at least 85 percent of their time, instead of applying good conduct to reduce their sentences to two-thirds. Most states have done away with this law.

Reinstatement of rehabilitation as priority

To eliminate much of the waste in our criminal justice system—human, social, moral, and financial waste—we need to return to making rehabilitation priority number one priority. This shift in public opinion promotes reducing incarceration of non-violent offenders and increasing alternative means of rehabilitation.

Relocation of female inmates

In February 2006, California Governor Arnold Schwarzenegger proposed moving 40 percent of the state's non-violent female inmates into neighborhood correctional centers, a plan that could help ease the state's severely overcrowded penitentiaries. The plan would allow about 4,500 female inmates to live closer to their families and receive job training and drug and alcohol counseling. No indication how much the relocation program would cost or if the neighborhood correctional centers already exist or would need building.

12

A Model Prison

*In 3,000 years of western history,
we have never gotten safe by being tough.*

James Gilligan
Harvard Researcher

There are several critical reasons why Thomson Correctional Center should open:

- It makes good fiscal sense.

- It reduces the critical problem of overcrowding.

- It alleviates countless problems associated with overcrowding.

- It stimulates the Illinois economy

- It lowers the unemployment rate in Carroll County.

If we could make Thomson a model prison, what would it be like? We tapped Charles Lockert, a former lifer who had served almost 30 years in state prisons, to come up with a model prison, which would aim to achieve the following goals: eliminate waste, minimize taxpayer burden, rehabilitate prisoners, and become virtually self-sustaining.

To understand how this model prison would work, we offer categories relative to the prison structure and note how, in each category, changes would be made to effect a more cost-effective prison.

Motto
ENTER & EXIT – ONE TIME

Prison employees

In most, if not all, of today's state corrections systems, nepotism is a common mode of employment. Many employees are unqualified or marginally qualified. Plucked from mines and farms, they often have little education and few cognitive skills for a job that demands both. They are ill equipped to deal with prisoners of cultures other than their own.

In our model prison, all employees would be required to have, at minimum, a two-year college degree to give the prison an educated base to deal with the daily challenges of operating a prison. Employees would earn $16/hour with incentives based on performance. Today many prison employees make $11/hour or less.

All prison employees would undergo background checks before being hired. They would be required to wear an ID badge equipped with a computer microchip. If a case arose concerning drug trafficking, the computer could pinpoint all officer movement 24/7.

The core group of employees that would monitor computers for inmates and employees would also undergo security screenings prior to being hired. Ideally, employees in this group would have a college degree.

Inmate classification

The prison would house inmates classified by levels of offenses, Level I, II, III and IV. Level IV is the most severe. Inmates would not be segregated by classification level but would be housed together. Their wrist and ankle ID bracelets with microchips would tell the officers their name, classification, cell house, and other pertinent information. There would be no way for one prisoner to assume another prisoner's identity.

Level I prisoners, generally considered minimum security risk, could work outside the prison walls but return at the end of each work day. The computer could easily sort out all Level I prisoners for this function without the need to house them together in the same cell house for classification and identification purposes.

Inmates

For our model maximum-security prison, no offender under the age of 25 would be admitted. No gangs would be allowed. Cellblocks would be multi-cultural, and no two men of the same culture would be housed side by side. Occupancy would be one man per cell.

Instead of a system of control in which men are locked down for 23 hours per day, this prison would encourage pursuit of education and work-oriented skills that foster self-identity and growth.

Inmates, who do not have a GED, would be required to attend school half days and work half days. No prisoners would be allowed to remain on idle. [At some prisons today, 500 or more men in a single cell house are on idle. Sixty-percent might be on psychotropic drugs, taking their medications three times a day in lines that take three hours to process. These men remain on idle, because of their mental state, largely due to the effect drugs have on them. This problem arose when many states closed down mental health treatment facilities and turned their patients into "instant offenders" in state prisons.]

If an inmate is a two-time loser (returning to prison once after being released), he must do twice the work of other prisoners. If he is a three-time loser, he will not be re-admitted to this prison. He is wasting everyone's time and the taxpayers' money. He does not demonstrate a serious determination to reform himself and move on to a better life.

Good behavior would be based on a point system. If an inmate accumulates 50 points, for example, he would be entitled to more frequent visits by friends and family on his approved visitors list and enjoy conjugal visits, to help him establish long-lasting relationships and preserve the family unit.

If an inmate is single, accumulates 50 points, and has a woman on his approved visiting list for at least one year in an ongoing relationship, he may be granted conjugal visits. This would minimize pent-up sexual frustrations and illicit behavior among prisoners.

To eliminate drug and other contraband trafficking, all visitors would be screened. If there has been any association with drugs, that person would not be approved to visit an inmate in this prison. Familiarity breeds contempt. [The same screening applies to all employees.]

An added benefit to the pre-screening of all visitors would be occasional prison-sponsored programs, such as open houses or musical revues, allowing inmates to perform or interact with friends and family.

Education and labor

Education and work are the prisoners' primary resources, enabling them to broaden their minds beyond the confines of the prison walls. An idle mind truly is the devil's workshop. Learning industrial and technical skills prepare them to pursue careers when they are released. Working at meaningful tasks reinforces qualities that would become vital to leading productive lives in a free society later.

Prison should not be a replacement for slave labor, and private companies would not be permitted to engage inmates in this prison in such practices. Unions, as a rule, are against inmate labor, because it undercuts the wages paid to union workers and therefore takes jobs away from them.

Prisoners would receive fair pay credit for work. For example, a barber's prevailing wage is $13/hour. If the prisoner-barber works 40 hours a week, he would earn credits of $520/week or $27,190/year. If his room and board at the prison cost $22,000/year and that were deducted from his earnings, he would keep $5,190 to support his family or save for when he leaves prison to start a new life. This system would give prisoners an incentive to save money. [First, we would have to educate about 80 percent of them in how to manage money.]

This system must not be gulag slave labor, and it must not take money from prisoners that should not be taken (child support when the prisoner has no children, as we mentioned earlier). It must be a system that offers incentives for saving, so that the inmate has a nest egg when he leaves prison that he can use to start a new life and support his family.

By being productive worker in prison, the inmate will help reduce the costs of running a medium-security prison, for example, in Illinois. So, by the prison becoming more of a self-sustaining facility, instead of costing the taxpayers $40 to $50 million dollars every year, it will cost only $20 million a year. In the process, we have helped rebuild lives. The savings realized in the model prison could be used to open the maximum-security prison at Thomson.

Commissary

For the work they perform in the model prison, inmates would receive sufficient pay to give them full access to commissary. The commissary would be prison-owned to have absolute control over contents sold to inmates.

The commissary would allow inmates to purchase a TV, radio or a computer equipped with limited access to the Internet (educational Web sites only) and emailing capabilities limited only to people approved on their visiting list.

The commissary would stock such items as underwear, towels, toothbrushes, and toothpaste that could be donated by manufacturers as not-for-sale items, giving those companies a tax write-off and providing prisoners with the bare necessities, leaving them other earned income to meet food, toiletry, clothing, and other maintenance requirements.

Corrections officers

In this prison, we would eliminate the walking officer. The only time inmates would see an officer would be in times of trouble. There would be no interaction between officers and inmates, no familiarity that can lead to preferential treatment or excessive abuse.

Sensors and computers would control all movement by officers, staff, and inmates. Incredible technology today can specifically detect movement. Sensors in homes, for instance, can alert residents that one male or female—or more than one—has entered their home.

House rules

Upon arrival at the prison, each inmate would be given a book of rules. All inmates would be required to attend a two-week indoctrination class, at which time everything about their incarceration would be described.

All prisoners must attend school half a day and work half a day. When they return to their cells, they would perform their duties in the cell house only.

A point system would apply to all prisoners. The rationale behind this system: When prison staff is not dictating every move to prisoners, the prisoners think for themselves. Making decisions helps them preserve their self-identity.

Daily physical counts would be eliminated. All inmates would wear arm and ankle bracelets equipped with computer microchips to facilitate daily counts. Only officers of the prison could remove a bracelet, which can be worn in the shower or during any other activities.

Recreation

Except for free weights, which could be wielded as weapons, the model prison would provide stationary workout equipment and all the necessary equipment for basketball, volleyball, board games, computer games, and a swimming pool, which would to be used as a perk in the point system. The goal is not to make prison life better than life on the streets but to offer wholesome activities while prisoners work on restoring the whole person through education, work, health and fitness, and social interaction with others.

Rehabilitation

At the model prison, inmates have a one-shot opportunity. If they're willing to take a real shot at rehabilitation and reformation, they can make it here.

While it is true that you can lead a horse to water but you cannot make him drink, rehabilitation is a halfway project. Both prison staff and inmates have to pull out all the stops. There is no room for vindictive justice here. Men come to this prison as punishment, not for punishment. Their loss of freedom is sufficient punishment. If you question that, ask anyone who has served time.

Not every prisoner will be willing to participate in a rehabilitation effort. If a prisoner at the model prison proves to be unwilling, he would have to learn the hard way: Pelican Bay, Walla Walla or any another state penitentiary where officials enforce 23-hour/day lockdowns.

If an inmate receives 5 Class D disciplinary reports (for an untidy cell and other misdemeanors), he would be transferred to a lockdown facility. The same is true for other disciplinary violations:

4 Class C write-ups (for minor movement infractions, being late, and so on).

3 Class B reports (for petty theft, lying to staff, being where he is not supposed to be)

1 Class A write-up (for drugs, violence, murder, assault or rape).

Private enterprise

In addition to their school and regular work assignments, inmates may engage in crafts, artwork, and other entrepreneurial enterprises approved by the prison. The prison would open a gift shop in the visitor processing facility that would sell items made by prisoners, with profits being split between the prison and the inmates that contribute items to the shop.

Food service

Fundamental nutrition problems contribute to crime. The Health Research Institute at the Pfeiffer Treatment Center in Warrensville, Illinois concludes that a deficient diet is a major contributing factor in violence and bad behavior. The DOC must use this knowledge as a basis for its nutritional composition of menus for prisoners.

In most state prisons today, if a prisoner does not have money coming from approved outside sources to his personal account, he can barely survive on the insufficient amounts of food provided three times a day by the prison kitchen. Portion control is the latest means to keep the bottom line flush, yet all the while denying inmates sufficient nourishment.

At the model prison, however, organizations, food companies, and manufacturers would be invited to donate food staples. In the past, USDA-donated staples never made it to the prison population but were instead sold by prison employees for personal profit. This practice would not be permitted here.

Most of today's prisons generally deliver less than 2300 calories total for each inmate, leaving inmates more and more dependent on commissary foods, which do not provide proper nourishment. Sometimes the food is spoiled or otherwise inedible, further decreasing their daily sustenance and forcing them to live on high-sodium, high-cholesterol canned meats, prepared foods, and junk food sold by the commissary.

The bottom line, of course, is another burden on the taxpayers (friends and families) that must provide extra funds to the inmates' commissary accounts for supplemental food. This unfair financial burden on friends and families of inmates is double jeopardy, because their taxes have already gone toward the operation of the prison, which includes feeding inmates.

The model prison would substantially increase the quality of food and amount of calories, decreasing the inmates' dependence on junk food. In fact, foods offered through the prison-operated commissary would be a wider variety, including health foods and foods geared to various dietary concerns.

The bottom line

By eliminating waste at virtually every level of prison operation and by instituting rules governing proper conduct, the model prison could become self-sustaining in less than five years, except for utilities. By turning enough revenue, we would remove the financial burden from the taxpayers and rely only minimally on tax dollars for those products and services that the prison cannot produce.

A self-sustaining prison provides a win-win situation for everyone concerned. For prison officials, it gives them greater control over their own destiny. For the inmates, it gives them a greater sense of self-identity and self-worth and prepares them for a better chance at a productive life upon release. For the taxpayers, it removes heavy reliance and opens doors for financial support of education and other meaningful social programs.

13

DISCUSSION POINTS

Our resources are misspent, our
punishments too severe, our
sentences too long.

Anthony M. Kennedy
Justice, U.S. Supreme Court
August 9, 2003

In *American Gulag*, we have presented many of the problems facing our criminal justice system: problems that have little hope of fading any time soon, problems of wasteful spending that show few signs of abating. In fact, some of these problems are growing worse year after year with shifting public demands, political rhetoric, and media hype.

At the end of each chapter, we have cited the issues of waste— financial, human, social, and moral—and throughout the book we have offered recommendations as to how to eliminate waste.

Now it is time to think outside the box. We have a critical need for a paradigm shift from the gulag warehousing/slave labor posture in today's criminal justice system to one that focuses on therapeutic justice, reformation, and peaceful, productive reentry into society.

Following are discussion points that hopefully will foster public dialogue, increase public participation in community programs for prisoners, and effect meaningful changes in the system that, at the present time, seems headed for a disastrous collision. These points are for discussion only and are not endorsed by the authors

Discussion Points

- Decriminalize drug possession

- Reinstate Pell grants for prisoners to pursue education

- Abolish prison sentences for non-violent drug offenders

- Institute oversight and accountability of privately managed prisons, healthcare providers, and food service

- Launch aggressive drug prevention programs

- Offer incentives for good behavior, education, job achievement

- Require anger management, conflict resolution, and tolerance classes in prisons for officers and prisoners alike

- Abolish the practice of housing non-violent offenders with hard-core criminals serving life sentences

- Develop meaningful ways to preserve the family unit while one member is in prison by encouraging family visits and treating families with respect with they visit the prison.

- Offer parenting classes to prisoners to help them better relate to their children and understand the extra burden placed on family members charged with childcare in their absence.

- Increase opportunities for inmates to handle their own day-to-day activities and make appropriate decision concerning them

- Work with prisoners to develop pro-social behavioral patterns

- Concentrate on treating the whole prisoner, attending to his basic needs (humane housing, adequate clothing, nutritional food, and standard healthcare), his economic needs (education and job skills transferable to the outside), his psychological needs (through programs that target his problem areas, such as anger and abuse of every kind), and his spiritual needs (encouraging religious practice and participation).

- Support political candidates that propose to work toward reforming our prison system and increasing efforts to rehabilitate prisoners while they are incarcerated and after they are released

- Donate to such organizations that offer viable alternatives to prison and help prisoners reintegrate following release

- Volunteer time, talents, and expertise to help community-based organizations.

- Eliminate prison sentences for some property and drug offenses.

- Remove the prison option for minor felonies.

- Support political candidates that advocate reform parole and probation practices to help ex-offenders assimilate better into society, eat nutritionally, work, support their families, and pursue education

- Eliminate post-release supervision for non-serious, non-violent, non-drug-sales offenders.

- Foster mentoring in prison.

- Become a volunteer literacy teacher.

- Emphasize multicultural and bilingual programs in schools, beginning with the very young.

- Recognize that the majority of offenders were not born to be criminals.

- Support organizations that return offenders to the community through training and reintegration programs (examples: Citizens for Effective Justice, Center for Therapeutic Justice, and many others across the country)

- Reopen mental health facilities or house mentally ill prisoners in separate units from the general prison population

- Enhance the education of corrections officers to include cognitive skills and basic counseling techniques, so they serve as more than caretakers

- Encourage colleges and universities to provide instructors on-site or by teleconferencing and computers to help prisoners advance their own education

- Adopt zero-based budgets in criminal justice systems, where the DOC commissioner would request each of his prison facilities to start with zero and justify every dollar he's asking to spend that year.

- Become outraged at the waste of tax dollars, lives, and human potential in our criminal justice system.

- Train inmates to become bakers, barbers, cooks, mechanics, and in other occupations that translate to the outside world.

- Put a courtroom in each prison to reduce overtime and risk of escape when transferring prisoners to and from courthouses.

- Train prisoners to become medical aides to assist in care-giving of the growing elderly population

- House elderly, infirm prisoners in minimum-security facilities that require fewer personnel and less costly security measures.

If you see an injustice and say nothing,
you have taken the side of the oppressor.

Bishop Desmond Tutu

Resources

Aborn, Richard M. March 4, 2005. "Time to End Recidivism". The Nation. www.thenation.com.

Abramsky, Sasha. July 10, 2001. "Breeding Violence". Debt to Society. Mother Jones. www.motherjones.com.

AFSCME Resolution: "Opposing prison privatization". June 26, 2000. www.afscme.org/about/resolute/2000/

Associated Press. January 8, 2003. "In Illinois, Pennsylvania, Wisconsin, newly built prisons remain shut, as states face budget crunch". www.justicepolicy.org/

Associated Press. October 4, 2001. "Recidivism rate steady in ⊠90-⊠00. Detroit Free Press.

Beiser, Vince. July 10, 2001. "How We Got to Two Million" Debt to Society. Mother Jones. www.motherjones.com.

Bernstein, Nell. July 10, 2001. "Left Behind". Debt to Society. Mother Jones. www.motherjones.com.

Bock, Audie. October 7, 2003. "Saving $1 billion a year by fixing the criminal justice system." www.smartvoter.org.

Bureau of Justice Statistics. Recidivism. Criminal Offenders. http://www.ojp.usdoj.gov/bjs/crimoff.htm.

Bureau of Justice Statistics. 2000. Mental Health Treatment in State Prisons. www.ojp.usdog.gov.

Bureau of Justice Statistics. 2001. State Prison Expenditures www.ojp.usdoj.gov.

Bureau of Justice Statistics. Education and Correction Populations. www.ojp.usdoj.gov

Bureau of Justice Statistics. June 30, 2003. Learn About Reentry.

Bureau of Justice Statistics. June 30, 2003. Prison statistics. www.ojp.usdoj.gov

Butterfield, Fox. July 25, 2004. "U. S. 'Correctional Population' Hits New High." The New York Times.

Carrillo, Silvio. June 13, 2000. "Should mandatory minimum sentencing laws be repealed?" www.speakout.com.

Center for Therapeutic Justice. August 2002. Williamsburg, Va. www.therapeuticjustice.com.

Christoff, Chris. July 21, 2004. "Michigan Prisons Could Swell Over New Gun Rules." The Detroit Free Press. www.freep.com.

Citizens for Effective Justice. Bloomington, Indiana. www.newleaf-cej.org.

Colorado Criminal Justice Reform Coalition.

Correctional Association of New York. Overview. www.correctionalassociation.org

Criminal Justice: Finland. Bureau of Justice Statistics. www.ojp.usdoj.gov/bjs/pub/ascii/wfbcfin.txt.

Curtis, Kim. January 18, 2006. "Prison rape study disputed." Associated Press. Detroit Free Press.

Cusac, Anne-Marie. July 10, 2001. "What's the Alternative?" Debt to Society. Mother Jones. www.motherjones.com.

"Cutting Correctly: New Prison Policies of Times of Fiscal Crisis". 2003. Justice Policy Institute. www.justicepolicy.org.

Dyer, Joel. 2000. *The Perpetual Prisoner Machine*. Boulder, CO: Westview Press.

Eggert, David. October 26, 2005. "Parole Pushed for Juvenile Offenders". AP/The Detroit Free Press.

Elsner, Alan. 2004. *Gates of Injustice*. New York: Prentice Hall.

Gerritt, Jeff. January 9, 2006. "Clothing industry would be a good fit for state prisons." Editorial. Detroit Free Press.

Hoge, Warren. January 2, 2003. "Finnish Prisons: No Gates or Armed Guards". The New York Times. www.nytimes.com.

Insight Prison Project. www.insightprisonproject.org.

Jackson, Jesse L., Sr. July 10, 2001. "Liberty & Justice for Some". Debt to Society. Mother Jones. motherjones.com.

"Jail Time". January 2006. Editorial. Detroit Free Press.

Johnson, Gov. Gary E. (R-NM). July 10, 2001. "Bad Investment." Debt to Society. Mother Jones. motherjones.com.

Justice Policy Institute. January 8, 2003. "In Illinois, Pennsylvania & Wisconsin, newly built prisons remain shut, as states fear budget crunch".

Kaiser, Robert G. September 25, 2005. "Why can't we be more like Finland?" The Seattle Times.

Kennedy, Anthony M. August 9, 2003. Speech. American Bar Association Annual Meeting.

Kerle, Ken. February 2006. American Jails. Personal interview.

Kobrin, Sandra. June 26, 2005. "Dying on our dime". Los Angeles Times. www.latimes.com.

Kocal, Thomas. 2005. "Open the Thomson Prison". Comprehensive Economic Development Strategy Focus Group.

Kominstkey, Diane M. "Prison, region shot down again. No funds, no negotiations for Thomson." Thomson, IL: Prairie Advocate.

Lamont, Matthew. "Government & the Prison System: A Mirror Image of Uselessness". www.breakthechains.net

"Learn about Reentry". 2004. U. S. Department of Justice.

Levitt, Steven D. and Stephen J. Dubner. 2005. *Freakonomics.* New York: William Morrow.

Lockert, Charles Edward. 2006. Personal interview.

McAdam, Douglas A. 2005. Personal interview. "Michigan Legislature Repeals Draconian Mandatory Minimum Drug Sentences". December 2002. www.criticalresistance.org.

Menninger, Karl. 1969. *The Crime of Punishment.* New York: Viking Compass Edition.

Michigan Prisoner Re-Entry Initiative. State of Michigan. www.michigan.gov/corrections.

Milford, Chris. January 2006. Personal interview.

Miller, Jerome G. Fall 2000. "American Gulag." www.yesmagazine.org.

Milliken, Governor William G. February 2006. Personal interview.

Moss, Carl. December 2005. Personal interview.

Moss, Morgan. January 2006. Personal interview. Williamsburg, Virginia. Center for Therapeutic Justice.

Muller, Eli. January 16, 2003. "More schools? Uh-uh, more prisons". Yale Daily News. www.yaledailynews.com.

Musgrave, Charles. 2006. Personal interview.

O'Connor, John. June 5, 2004. "Locked up on prisons— State agonizes over closings". Associated Press.

O'Leary, John. 1993. "Private involvement in public corrections profits, pros, cons, and convicts." Perspectives on the Professions. Los Angeles, California.

Lawrence Bruckner & Luanne Bruckner

Parenti, Christian. September 1, 1999. "The Prison Industrial Complex: Crisis and Control". www.corpwatch.org.

Patton, Zach. April 2005. "Contract Lens." Governing Magazine. http:// governing.com/archive/2005/apr/prison.txt

Penal Colony. http://en.wikipedia.org

"Prison Brief for the United States of America". 2005. London: International Centre for Prison Studies.

"Prison, Region shot down again—No Funds, no negotiations for Thomson". Prairie Advocate News.

Prison Build Program. www.michigan.gov/corrections.

Prison Overcrowding. www.johnhoward.ab.ca

Prison Service: Finland. www.vankeinhoito.fi/14994.htm

"Prison Waste". www.prisoners.com

Rasmussen, Kristina. August 22, 2005. "Taxpayers Should Not Be Shackled to Empty Prisons". Human Events. www.humaneventsonline.com.

Reinhart, Tanya. June 30, 2002. "The Penal Colonies". Yediot Aharonot. www.tau.ac.il.

Rossi, Richard. "Public Humiliation". www.ccadp.org.

Rossi, Richard. December 2003. "Prison Overcrowding in Arizona". www.ccadp.org.

Royse, David. October 9, 2005. "Troubles Abound in Florida Prisons." AP/The Miami Herald.

Rubitschun, John. June 9, 2005. "Parole: The issues, concerns". Detroit Free Press.

Rutherford, Dan. May 9, 2005. Letter to Editor. Chicago, IL: The Chicago Tribune.

Sarche, Jon. 2005. "Law officials seek sentencing changes". The Deseret News. Associated Press. www.famm.org.

Showalter, Dr. Stanley. January 2006. Personal interview.

Silverstein. Ken. June 1, 1997. "America's Private Gulag." CorpWatch. www.corpwatch.org/

Smith, Phil. Fall 1993. Private Prisons: Profits of Crime. Covert Action Quarterly. mediafilter.org/caq/Prison.html.

Soering, Jens. 2004. *An Expensive Way to Make Bad People Worse*. New York: Lantern Books.

Street, Paul. March 4, 2003. "Mass incarceration and racist state priorities at home and abroad". www.zmag.org/

Study: mandatory minimum drug sentences don't work. May 12, 1997. Washington, DC: CNN. www.cnn.com.

Taylor, Rev. Hal. January 20, 2006. Personal Interview.

Telford, John. January 25, 2002. "Rehabilitation and job training aid in transition." Detroit Free Press.

Times of India. April 30, 2005. "One in Every 138 Americans is Behind Bars". timesofindia.indiatimes.com.

Tuhus-Dubrow, Rebecca. December 19, 2003. "Prison Reform Talking Points." The Nation. www.thenation.com.

United States Supreme Court, Washington, D. C.

Wagner, Peter. 2003. "Finland: Crime Control & Decarceration." The Prison Index: Taking the Pulse on the Crime Control Industry. Published by the Western Prison Project.

Walker, Roger E. Jr. October 7, 2005. Letter from the Director. "Illinois Department of Corrections—2003 Statistical Presentation". www. idoc.state.il.us/

Weed, William Speed. July 10, 2001. "Incubating Disease. Debt to Society". Mother Jones. www.motherjones.com.

"What is 'Judges Against the Drug War'?" www.judgesagainstthedrugwar. org.

Wilkinson, Reginald A., Ed.D. August 21, 2004. "Prison jobs teach inmates skills, instill work ethic." Columbus Dispatch.

Wrongful Death Institute. June 30, 2003. Prison Statistics. www. wrongfuldeathinstitute.com.

Yee, Daniel. December 9, 2005. "Inmate cleared by DNA is set free". Associated Press. Detroit Free Press.

Zoroya, Gregg. July 2004. "Smoking bans spread to prisons". USA TODAY. www.usatoday.com.

.

www.ingramcontent.com/pod-product-compliance
Lightning Source LLC
Chambersburg PA
CBHW020251290526
45784CB00003B/1192